Guide to High-Performance Investing

By the Editors of
Investor's Business Daily

Cover design by Steve Hodowsky

Printed in the United States of America

by

O'Neil Data Systems, Inc.
12655 Beatrice Street
Los Angeles, California 90066-7003

1   2   3   4   5   6   7   8   9   0

Contents

III. Stock Analysis

IV. Investment Strategy

V. Mutual Funds

Preface

When asked what *Investor's Business Daily* has that other newspapers don't, I often have to stop and think. It's not that examples don't readily come to mind. It's that there are so many I don't know where to begin. So, I often find myself answering: "How much time do I have?"

On such occasions I'm also reminded how formidable a task it is for readers to understand all that's in the paper and how to use it to their advantage. Over the years, we've produced various pamphlets, tapes and books to help with the learning process. But the questions keep coming.

In the paper itself, we've run two series of explanatory features—one in 1987-88 called "Inside *Investor's Daily*" and the other in 1989-90 called "Educating Investors" (a feature we resumed in late 1992). We got a lot of positive feedback on both series, and many readers have asked for reprints.

This book is a compilation of many articles from those series. We've made a special effort to include articles on those features in the paper that generate the most questions, such as how to interpret the "Psychological Market Indicators" on the General Market Indicators page.

Most of the articles were written by Leo Fasciocco, dean of U.S. stock-market writers, who also writes our daily "Inside the Market" column on NYSE action. Examples used in his original stories have been updated where necessary. The charts are by Alan Hoffman, our graphics editor.

We hope these articles—many of which include insights from

America's top market analysts and money managers—will help make *Investor's Business Daily* even more useful to our already loyal readers.

If there is other information you need, or improvements you would like to see in *Investor's Business Daily*, please let us know. We get thousands of suggestions each year. All are given serious consideration, and many find their way into the paper or our other products.

Wesley F. Mann
Editor

General Market Indicators

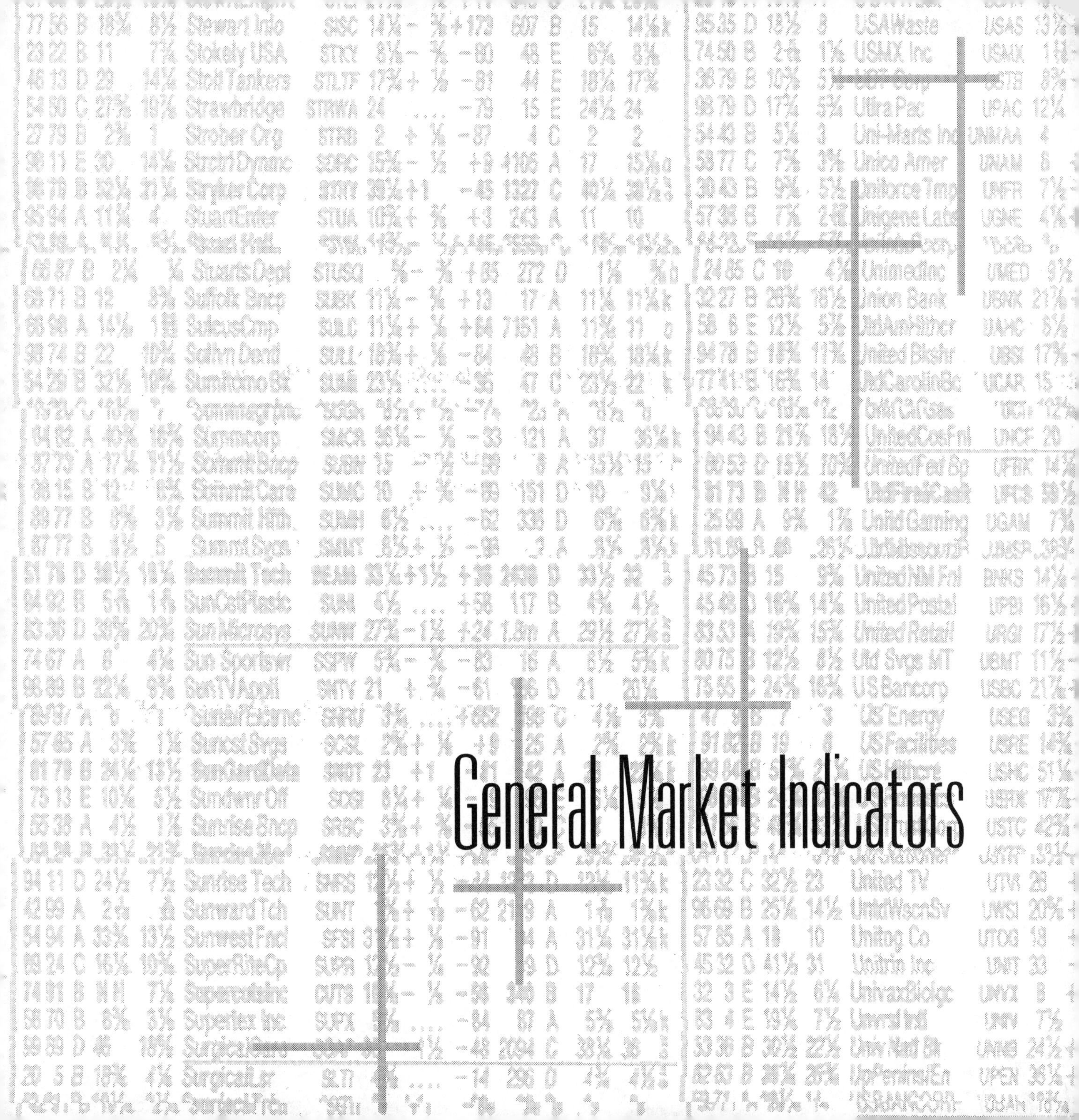

Market Indexes

Fingers On The Pulse Of The Broad Market

■ **Knowing if you're in a bull market or a bear market solves half the problem in selecting stocks.**

In the world of stock market investing, a lot of cliches get tossed around. Among the classics: "Don't fight the tape" and "the trend is your friend."

As with most cliches, these one-liners contain more than a shred of truth, especially when it comes to market activity. Experienced investors have come to know that the general trend of the overall market has a major influence on the performance of individual issues.

Knowing if you're in a bull market (rising prices) or bear market (declining prices), or even a choppy market (sideways pattern with volatility), solves half the problem in selecting stocks.

Many experts believe that proper analysis of the market's trend is 60% of the process of selecting winning stocks.

Because most investors buy long, as opposed to selling short, it's important to be aware of the difference between market corrections—5% to 10% declines in an otherwise rising long-term trend—and dreaded bear markets.

It's been said that in a bear market at least three of four stocks will fall. Another cliche is appropriate here: "When they raid the house, they get them all."

Analyzing The Market

There are many ways to analyze the stock market. *Investor's Business Daily* doesn't promote any particular method. But knowing the importance of market data, the newspaper has provided its readers with a wealth of information and an attractive

Stock Market Indexes

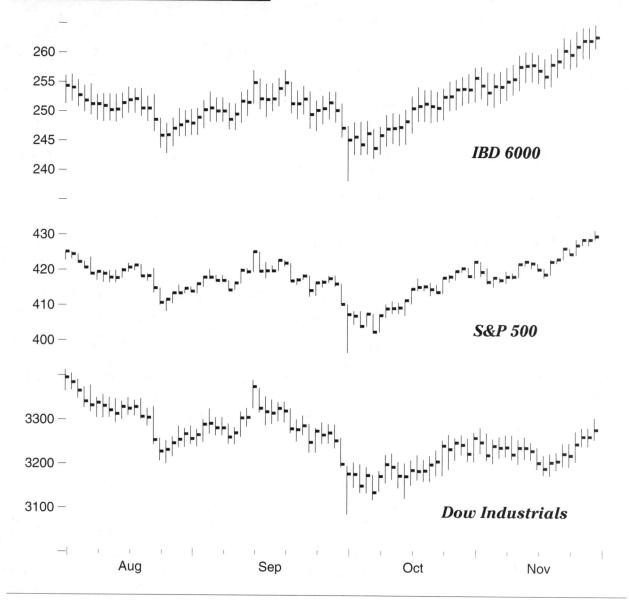

IBD 6000

S&P 500

Dow Industrials

Aug   Sep   Oct   Nov

layout of market indexes to give investors a bearing on where the market has been, where it is now and where it may be going in the future.

Investor's Business Daily's display of the most important indexes appears every day on the "General Market Indicators" page. The broad indexes shown there span a nine-month period—providing a far wider, and therefore a more meaningful, perspective than those found in other newspapers.

The major market indexes covered are (1) the *Investor's Business Daily* Stock Index of 6,000 issues traded on the New York Stock Exchange, the American Stock Exchange and the Over-The-Counter market; (2) the Standard & Poor's composite of 500 stocks, and (3) the Dow Jones average of 30 industrial issues.

The indexes are stacked one on top of another so the reader can detect any "divergences." Divergences occur when some indexes are moving higher while others are not. This is sometimes a tip-off of a change in the trend of the market.

The charts on the facing page show four months of market action in the fall of 1992, a period when the Dow industrial average lagged while the broader market, and especially the smaller stocks that the broad *Investor's Business Daily* 6000 includes, did much better.

The *Investor's Business Daily* 6000, for example, was the first to move back into record territory (in early November), while the Dow remained nearly 200 points below its previous high.

Subindex Charts

Below the main charts on the "General Market Indicators" page are smaller charts of subindexes that show how various sectors of the market are doing.

These include the NYSE and Nasdaq composite indexes and the Dow transportation and utilities averages. They also include a variety of proprietary *Investor's Business Daily* indexes on key sectors of the U.S. economy such as Junior Growth, High-Technology, Consumer, Defensive, Medical-Health Care

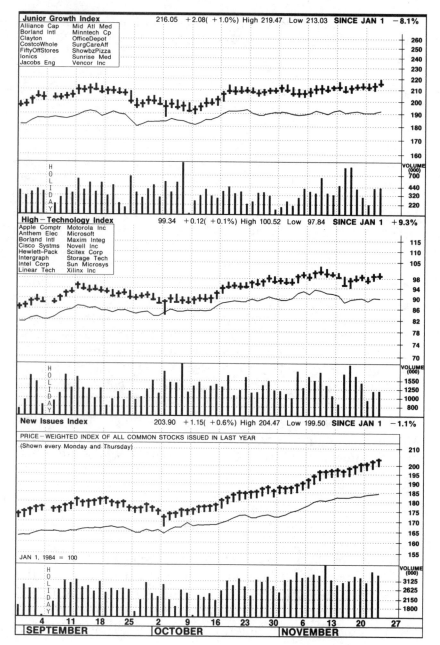

Junior Growth Index   216.05   +2.08(+1.0%) High 219.47 Low 213.03 **SINCE JAN 1** −8.1%

Alliance Cap	Mid Atl Med
Borland Intl	Minntech Cp
Clayton	OfficeDepot
CostcoWhole	SurgCareAff
FiftyOffStores	ShowbzPizza
Ionics	Sunrise Med
Jacobs Eng	Vencor Inc

VOLUME (000)

High − Technology Index   99.34   +0.12(+0.1%) High 100.52 Low 97.84 **SINCE JAN 1** +9.3%

Apple Comptr	Motorola Inc
Anthem Elec	Microsoft
Borland Intl	Maxim Integ
Cisco Systms	Novell Inc
Hewlett−Pack	Scitex Corp
Intergraph	Storage Tech
Intel Corp	Sun Microsys
Linear Tech	Xilinx Inc

VOLUME (000)

New Issues Index   203.90   +1.15(+0.6%) High 204.47 Low 199.50 **SINCE JAN 1** −1.1%

PRICE − WEIGHTED INDEX OF ALL COMMON STOCKS ISSUED IN LAST YEAR

(Shown every Monday and Thursday)

JAN 1, 1984 = 100

VOLUME (000)

| 4 | 11 | 18 | 25 | 2 | 9 | 16 | 23 | 30 | 6 | 13 | 20 | 27 |
| **SEPTEMBER** | | | | **OCTOBER** | | | | **NOVEMBER** | | | | |

and New Issues. These charts include Relative Strength lines showing how each sector is doing compared to the overall market (S&P 500).

These charts provide important clues to what's working in the market and what is not.

The charts on this page are from the Nov. 27, 1992, edition. They show how, for one example, new issues (stocks that had come public over the prior 12 months) were clearly outperforming the market. (By the end of November, some issues were doubling in their first day of trading.)

Moving Averages

Smoothing Out Broad Market Trends

The basic rule is that if an index is moving *decisively* above or below its 200-day average, it will act as a buy or sell signal.

In the fall of 1992, the Dow Jones industrial average was meandering below its 200-day moving average, the Standard & Poor's 500 index was riding just above its 200-day line but the Nasdaq composite index was soaring high above its moving average.

The message, according to many technical analysts, was that smaller-cap growth stocks—most of which trade on the Nasdaq—were where it was at.

"Although there will be corrections along the way, the (Nasdaq's) the area to be in," Stan Weinstein, publisher of *The Professional Tape Reader*, a Hollywood, Fla.-based newsletter, said at the time.

"Conversely," he added, "with the Dow below its moving average, blue chips and other big-cap stocks may not be the place to be."

Subsequent market action bore him out, as the broader market indexes, including the Nasdaq composite, soon climbed to new highs while the Dow Jones industrial average lagged behind.

Long-Term Trends

How could Weinstein and others have been so sure?

The 200-day moving average (calculated by averaging the closing prices for the past 200 trading days) is a long-term trend indicator that smooths out choppy day-to-day trading activity and clarifies market direction. It is most useful for longer-term

Stock Market Indexes

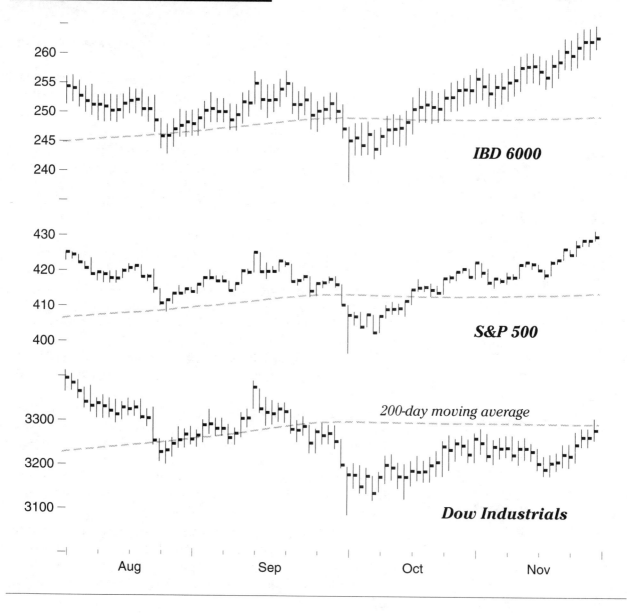

IBD 6000

S&P 500

200-day moving average

Dow Industrials

Aug   Sep   Oct   Nov

investors. Many shorter-term moving averages are also tracked closely by analysts.

Investor's Business Daily is the only newspaper that provides moving averages.

To help readers assess the direction of the overall market, 200-day moving average lines are plotted daily for the Dow industrials, the S&P 500 and the *Investor's Business Daily* 6000 indexes, for the Nasdaq composite, the American Stock Exchange's Market Value index and the *Investor's Business Daily* Mutual Fund Index.

For individual stocks, 200-day lines are provided for companies that appear in the daily "Industries in the News" feature, and 50-day moving average lines are plotted for each of the 90 "Stocks in the News" charts.

The most basic rule of thumb in working with any moving average is that "if an index is moving decisively above or below its 200-day moving average line, it will more often than not act as a buy or sell signal," explained Ricky Harrington, market strategist at Marion Bass Securities Inc. in Charlotte, N.C.

But it's also important to remember that moving averages are just one of many tools that technical analysts use to gauge market conditions.

"You can't take one technical indicator and act on it in a vacuum," warned Marc Chaikin, senior vice president of Instinet Corp. in New York. "That's not prudent."

"Mechanical" Technical Tools

Moving averages fall in the category of "mechanical" technical tools. The two other major areas of analysis are the psychological indicators (or market sentiment data) and fundamentals, which relate to such factors as the economy, interest rates and earnings.

The first step in analyzing a moving average is determining whether a market index—such as the Dow or S&P 500—is above or below its moving average line. When an index moves above the line, it's positive. When it moves below it, it's negative.

Some regard moving averages as "lagging" indicators that can be dangerously late in giving buy or sell signals.

Watching for divergences between key market indexes and their moving averages can be helpful. When the major market indexes are above their 200-day moving averages and one suddenly drops below it, the other market averages will often follow, says Chaikin.

Investors should also keep an eye on the slope of the moving average line, says Weinstein.

It's healthy, he says, "if the average is rising relatively sharply and (the index) is well above it. If the moving average is essentially flat and the market (index) is above it, that's OK, but not as healthy as if the moving average is rising and the index is above it."

Conversely, he says, "if an index is below a sharply declining moving average, that's a negative situation."

Breaking Through

Take particular notice when an index violates its moving average after being above or below it for a long time. "That's usually a sign of change in the trend for the market," says Weinstein. "If an index is above its moving average for a long time and then breaks below it, that means the market is topping out.

"Conversely, if it is below the moving average for a long time and finally edges above it, that means the market is ready to change direction and go up."

Don Hays, director of investment strategy at Wheat, First, Butcher & Singer Inc. in Richmond, Va., recalls how the S&P 500, after riding above its 200-day line for more than three

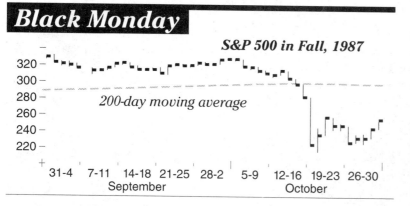

Black Monday

S&P 500 in Fall, 1987

320
300
280 — *200-day moving average*
260
240
220

31-4   7-11   14-18   21-25   28-2   5-9   12-16   19-23   26-30
September   October

Mutual Fund Index

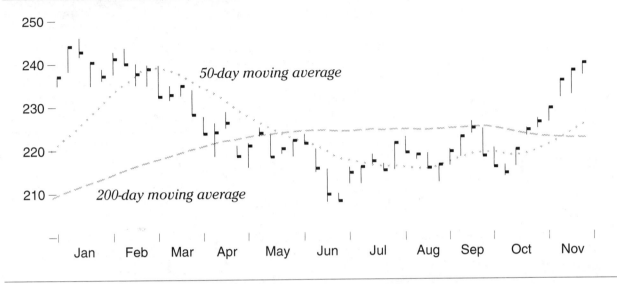

years, knifed below it on the Thursday before Black Monday in October 1987.

After three solid years of advancing markets, that move was a clear warning sign, said Hays. He says it also was part of the catalyst that spurred the crash.

Mere penetration of the 200-day line, however, is no guarantee of a change in market direction.

On Sept. 14, the Nasdaq composite poked its head above its 200-day average as it extended a three-week rally. But it retreated the very next session and sold off the rest of the month.

In early October, the Nasdaq started to rally again and accompanied by very heavy volume moved back above its 200-day line by mid-month. It was been up, up and away for the Over-The-Counter market after that.

Because there is no definitive way to read the violation of a moving average line, "an investor must always put technical patterns in the context of his fundamental view," advises Chaikin.

"If you're bullish on the market fundamentally and underinvested and you see a segment of market you're interested in move above its moving average on heavy volume that technical condition, combined with (a positive) fundamental view, should be a buy signal."

But "if your view of the fundamental picture is negative," he added, "you might just watch the market more closely at that point to see if in fact the penetration of the average on the upside" is significant. If the index continues higher, it may be a good time to rethink your market view.

If you're bearish and the market cuts below its moving average, it's a loud sell signal. If you're bullish, caution may be in order.

If all this seems confusing, it is.

"Tracking moving averages takes persistence and a lot of hard work," said Harrington. "It also requires some intuition and a bit of luck."

Keep in mind that moving averages, like all indicators, are not infallible. There are times when an index will whipsaw back and forth through its moving average. In this case, it's hard to reach any conclusions, said Harrington.

But when its direction is clear, a moving average can be very useful because, Harrington noted, "the cardinal rule in investing is to buy stocks in uptrends and sell them in downtrends."

Advance-Decline Lines

Staying In Sync With Market's Real Trend

■ **Investors who heeded the A-D line's warnings avoided the October 1987 market plunge.**

The stock market is a battle in which bulls are pitted against bears. Knowing who has the upper hand—and making sure you're on the same side—can help you make money and avoid costly mistakes.

Among the technical tools that keep you in sync is the advance-decline line.

If those stocks moving up outnumber those moving down, the market is improving and considered bullish. If more stocks are declining, the market is in retreat and the bears have gained the advantage.

The concept is simple. But how should an investor interpret the action of the advance-decline line in relation to other indicators?

Gainers Vs. Losers

Market technicians produce an advance-decline line by taking all New York Stock Exchange stocks that rise in price for the day and subtract those that fall. Stocks that close unchanged are not used.

The difference of daily advances vs. declines is added to a running tally. If the advance-decline difference is negative, the result is subtracted from the cumulative total. An advance-decline figure is then plotted so a trend can be observed.

The same technique is used to derive a weekly advance-decline line. Some analysts favor a weekly advance-decline line because it removes some of the volatility.

Forecasting Market Tops

The advance-decline line has an impressive track record of forecasting major market tops.

Investors who heeded its warnings avoided the October 1987 market plunge of 1,000 points in the Dow Jones industrial average. They also avoided holding long positions during the 1973 to 1974 bear market that sent the Dow tumbling from 1036 to 578.

Investor's Business Daily is the only daily newspaper that provides advance-decline lines. They appear in the "General Market Indicators" section.

Analysts often refer to the market's "breadth." If the widely followed Dow industrials rise sharply, but advances lead declines by only a slim margin, analysts will say breadth is weak. If the Dow is up only slightly but advances overwhelm declines, they'll say breadth is strong.

Some analysts also construct advance-decline lines for the Nasdaq, American Stock Exchange and various market sectors, including medical, computer or retail stocks.

Using The A-D Line

When analyzing an advance-decline line, try to detect its trend (up or down), the pattern of its highs and lows (is each high higher than the last, for example?) and any divergences from market averages.

Looking at the 1992 advance-decline above, you can see, for example, the trend was higher from early October.

Some money managers put a spin on the A-D line. Robert Walsh, of Jenswold King & Associates in Houston, will use the A-D information to plot a 10-day (short-term) or 30-day (intermediate-term) moving average. If the trend is above the moving average line, it's bullish. If it's below, that's bearish.

A pattern of higher highs and higher lows for the daily A-D line can be seen since October. This, too, is bullish. A violation of the pattern (a high that didn't exceed the last high and/or a

Advance-Decline Line

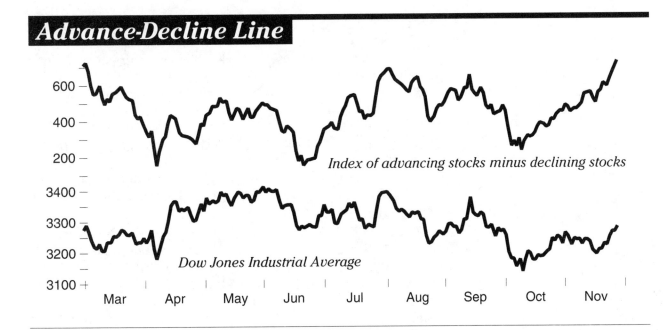

Index of advancing stocks minus declining stocks

Dow Jones Industrial Average

low that is lower than the last low) would send up a warning flare.

Most interestingly, the A-D line showed a bullish divergence because the Dow industrial average was moving sideways. That indicated the market was a lot stronger than the Dow suggested.

The A-D line helps to warn of market tops because it will sometimes turn down ahead of the Dow.

In May and in early June of 1992, the Dow rallied to new-high ground, but the A-D line did not. While the "generals" (in the blue-chip average) were advancing, in other words, the "troops" (most other stocks) were deserting. The result: bulls were routed, driving the A-D line still lower and sending the Dow into a 200-point retreat.

The lesson: Always be careful when new highs made by the Dow or S&P 500 are not confirmed by the broad market in the form of an improving A-D line. The reason the A-D line fails in these cases is that certain sectors of the market are beginning to deteriorate.

Generally, this key pattern of divergence occurs near the end of a bull market because:

- Certain sectors of stocks head lower because they begin to discount the end of the business upturn six to nine months in advance.
- Utility stocks weaken because of a rise in interest rates.
- The blue chips are the last to be sold because people are still enchanted by the market and reluctant to sell the big names because they are dominant companies in their industries.

The A-D line isn't as helpful in signaling market bottoms. One reason is that the Dow, for instance, can respond more quickly to a change in events—such as a cut in the discount rate—because it's made up of only 30 stocks. The A-D line needs more time and broader buying to lure bearish investors back into the bullish column.

There are exceptions, however. In 1941-1942, the advance-decline line diverged bullishly from the Dow. In doing so, it acted as a harbinger of a strong and broad bull market that carried the Dow from 93 in 1943 to 213 in 1946.

Boldfacing In Stock Tables

Diagnosing The Market's Health By Its Pallor

■ **The market is strong when the tables have a blacker, snappier look.**

It can be frustrating when the stock market, as it did for much of 1991 and 1992, generally moves sideways without resolution up or down.

Analyst opinions fall all over the ballpark. There is even a tendency to overanalyze the situation. At such times, it can be instructive to step back, worry less about where the market might be headed next, and try to get a feel for what it's doing now.

There are many indicators available from a variety of sources that can help in this effort. Every investor and analyst seems to have his or her favorites.

One of the quickest ways to get a feel for the market is simply by turning through the pages of *Investor's Business Daily.* The newspaper contains many features you won't find anywhere else, and it may give you—simply from a glance—a better idea of what's going on.

One of the best, and easiest, ways is just to look at the stock tables themselves.

Like a doctor who can tell a lot by a patient's pallor, investors can get a feel for the condition of the market from the "color" of the tables.

Investor's Business Daily pioneered in the use of boldface type and other techniques to make stock tables more useful and time-saving. Specifically, we boldface stocks that made new highs and/or were up a point or more in the previous day's trading.

— C —

61	94	A	NH	11½	CBTFncl	CBTF	24	....	+436	632	2.5	24½	23¾k
68	24	A	8⅜	3 11/16	CBL Medical	CBLM	4 5/16	− 1/16	−17	211		4½	4¼
....	.		5⅛	NL	CBL wt	CBLMW	1¼	− 7/16	....	3		1¼	1¼
77	74	B	2 1/16	9/16	CCA Industr	CCAM	1 7/16	....	+73	314		1½	1⅜
81	56	B	36⅛	27⅝	CCB Fincial	CCBF	34⅜	+1⅜	+208	197	3.5	34½	33½
81	92	A	15¼	7	CCOR Electr	CCBL	15	....	−4	216		15¼	14¼
36	10	B	10½	3⅝	CESftwre	CESH	4⅜	+ ⅛	+19	198		4⅜	4⅛
54	20	B	15½	7	CEM Corp	CEMX	7⅞	....	−81	37		8	7⅞
6	52	.	NH	12½	CFBancorp	CFBC	14¾	− ¼	−69	46	.5	15⅛	14¾
71	97	A	NH	3	CFS Fincial	CFSC	13¾	+ ¼	+192	272		14¼	13
95	85	A	6⅞	3½	CIS Techlgy	CISI	6½	....	−22	1064		6⅝	6⅜
48	82	A	2¾	⅝	CMSData	LAWR	2⅛	....	−83	10		2⅛	2⅛
92	71	B	NH	20¾	CNB Bncshs	CNBE	29	+ ½	−45	21	3.2	29½	29
80	66	A	10¾	6¾	CPAC Inc	CPAK	9½	....	−87	12	2.7	9½	9½
80	31	B	27¼	22	CPB Inc	CPBI	23½	....	+886	217	3.4	23¾	23
96	97	B	25⅜	6⅜	CSF Holdings	CSFCB	23	....	−61	71		23½	23
97	78	D	10	6¼	CSP Inc	CSPI	9⅝	....	−80	19		10	9⅝
24	61	B	16¼	9¾	C TEC Corp	CTEX	13¼	−1¼	−19	86		13¾	13¼
38	17	A	6¾	3½	CU Bancorp	CUBN	4¾	+ ½	−99	1		4¾	4¾
22	28	B	16¾	6¼	Cabot Med	CBOT	10	+ ¾	+187	1126		10⅛	9¼
46	79	B	2⅝	1⅜	Cache Inc	CACH	2⅝	+ ⅜	+35	169		2⅝	2¼
43	34	B	5 15/16	3¼	CACI Intl Inc	CACI	4 1/16	− 1/16	+87	536		4¼	4 1/16
87	19	C	38⅜	26⅞	CadburySch	CADBY	27⅜	+ ⅛	−54	251	4.3	27⅜	27
48	2	E	2⅝	NL	Cade Indus	CADE	13/16	+ 1/32	+334	1368		13/16	23/32
70	33	A	10¼	5¾	CadmusCom	CDMS	9	+1⅜	+999	1421	2.2	9	8¼

Conversely, we underline those stocks that made new lows or were down a point or more.

These devices not only highlight individual stocks but also give the overall tables a certain look. The market is strong when the tables have a lot of boldfacing, which gives the tables a blacker, snappier look.

The excerpt at left from the Nasdaq stock tables in the Nov. 27, 1992, issue, a period when OTC stocks were rallying strongly. Six of the first 25 listings under "C" were boldfaced because they had either made news highs or gained a point or more the day before.

When the market is weak, there's a lack of boldfacing, giving the tables a duller, grayer look.

If the same listings at left were excerpted from the tables six months earlier—on May 27, 1992, when the market in general and the Nasdaq in particular were in a corrective phase—you would see no boldfacing at all.

In a bad bear market—or during a collapse as we had in 1987, when most stocks were underlined—the tables, like the market itself, look downright ugly.

Ticker Tape Reading

A Dying Art Still Critical To Some Analysts

■ **The ticker tape gives traders a feel for the emotion on the floor of the exchange.**

To the novice, the ticker tape is a blur of numbers and letters racing across a screen, but to many professionals it's a vital tool for successful trading.

The ticker tape is the up-to-the-minute rundown of individual stock trades from the floor of the New York Stock Exchange.

To professional tape readers, such as Trude Latimer of Wayne Grayson Capital Corp. in New York, it's an integral part of their trading. And following the tape is no easy task.

"Anyone can watch their own stocks cross the tape," says Latimer. "But that's not being a tape watcher. You need to watch the tape day in and day out, do your homework and then put it all together with a degree of instinct to come up with good investment ideas."

For starters, she says, traders should know about two-thirds of the 2,400 ticker symbols that make up the Big Board. Each trade crossing on the tape is made up of the stock symbol, the latest price (measured in eighths) and the amount of the stock traded (in hundreds of shares).

Price changes aren't included until after the close. During trading, it's up to the astute observer to remember the last trade.

Some companies' symbols are easy to remember, such as "GM" for General Motors Corp. and "IBM" for International Business Machines Corp. Others are less recognizable.

Each day, *Investor's Business Daily* publishes ticker symbols for each listed stock and most Over-The-Counter issues.

T $_{42s48^3/_4}$ **GM** $_{10s34^1/_2}$ WAG $_{24s43^1/_4}$ IC $_{100s24^3/_4}$ BFI $_{25^7/_8}$ JNJ $_{32s21^1/_8}$ AIT $_{10s65^1/_8}$ KSF $_{20s11^5/_8}$ S

ASKI $_{10s22^1/_8}$ GPAR $_{10s4^1/_8}$ ADLI $_{9^7/_8}$ TCOMA $_{8s21}$ CHKR $_{250s21}$ MWGP $_{24}$ SGAT $_{22}$ NSBA $_{16}$

In this example, the ticker tape of New York Stock exchange (on top) shows 1,000 shares of General Motors trading at $34.50 each. Below are Over-The-Counter transactions.

Also available, from the *Investor's Business Daily* library is a 60-page "Industry Group and Ticker Symbol Index." It shows the ticker symbol for every publicly held company plus its industry group.

The *Investor's Business Daily Almanac 1992*, also available from the library, includes a handy symbol guide arranged alphabetically by both company and symbol.

Using The Tape

Many brokerage firms used to operate "board rooms" where individuals could sit and watch the tape on an electronic scoreboard. But those are mostly a thing of the past.

Today, you can watch the tape crawling across the bottom of the television screen on certain business shows and local stations.

Eugene Peroni, an analyst with Janney Montgomery Scott Inc. in Philadelphia, is another who keeps a close eye on the tape. He has a 12-foot-long electronic display of the NYSE ticker tape in his office.

"It's wonderful and a big conversation piece," said Peroni, "But more important than that, it is the foundation of my technical analysis.

"I came into this business ago under my father's tutelage, and watching the ticker tape (then) was very important," he recalls. "In a way, it has fallen out of fashion because of computers. But I find the tape works well. It gives me a feel for the emotion on the floor of the exchange."

Each day before the market opens, Peroni reviews his charts and reads newspapers like *Investor's Business Daily* to be up on the news. He also follows closely the news on the Dow Jones News Service, which provides up-to-the-minute corporate information.

$7^3/_8$ USS $23s71^1/_2$ SLB $58^1/_8$ PDT $11^3/_8$ ARV $20s11^1/_8$ TOC $11^5/_8$ TDM $10s10^3/_8$ MFV $14^3/_4$ SPP $200s37$

AA $5s1^7/_{16}$ TGA $10s16^3/_4$ SYNT $50s5^3/_8$ SVGI $50s6^5/_8$ DELL $100s39^1/_2$ CMPX 7 NYT A $25^7/_8$ CANO 5

He then makes a special list of stocks he wants to watch that may be near what he calls "break points" from price bases. These would be potential buys.

He also has a list of stocks with stop points that might be sell candidates.

One of the things Peroni looks for on the tape is the spread between consecutive trades of the same stock.

For example, if a stock's last trade was 48 and the next 48 1/8, the spread would be 1/8. He finds that when savvy buyers are accumulating stock, the spread will be small but the volume and frequency of trades will pick up. That would be the time to buy.

When the spread opens to 1/4, 3/8 or even 1/2, Peroni says, the stock is telegraphing that it is becoming more widely known and people are buying it "at the market" at any cost. The buying, in other words, is becoming emotional.

That is not the time to "chase" the stock, he says. A good tape reader should have been in the stock before the runup action.

Signature Trading

Occasionally, Peroni can tell when a different specialist is handling a stock. Specialists are firms at the Big Board that must maintain an orderly market in specific stocks. A new or temporary specialist might permit a stock to become more volatile, and that's something Peroni can pick up.

Another thing both Peroni and Latimer look for is when a stock that hasn't been trading much starts to "paint the tape."

"The tape will reveal the seeds of a move," says Latimer. "One can see by looking at the tape when there is an increase in interest in a particular stock.

"Tape watching is an art, not so much a science," said Latimer. "I read papers and magazines to help me, but I don't take what I read literally. I try not to let opinions influence me.

"I keep my opinions pure and let the tape talk to me. Articles and rumors on stocks only provide background for me on why a stock might be up or down. I use it only in that I am aware that it exists."

Long-Term Positions

Both Peroni and Latimer note that buying and selling using the tape can be useful for trading in the short term, such as a few days. But they say that it also can be a good starting point for a longer-term position.

Latimer thinks it takes at least five years to become a good tape reader. The student should also go through the cycle of a bull and bear market. "The longer you watch, the better you become," she says. "It's like learning the personality of a thousand children.

"I don't find watching the tape tiring," she adds. "I am usually caught up in the excitement. There is always something going on. So, I am rarely bored."

Peroni echoes the sentiment. "Watching the tape builds wisdom," he says. "If I've been away from it for a vacation, it does take a few days to reorient myself, just like a tennis or golf pro needs time to get his timing back. But watching the tape is something I enjoy very much."

Ticker Tape Study

A Time-Saving Way To Monitor Buying And Selling

■ **Names that pop up on the up-tick list during the first stage of a major advance may turn out to be the market leaders.**

Although the old-fashioned ticker-tape machine with the glass bubble is now a museum piece, the numbers its modern counterparts produce are still crucial to investors, especially traders.

With eyes glued to wall-mounted electronic quote boards or computer screens, modern "tape-watchers" keep a lookout for a sudden pickup in turnover and/or price in a previously inactive stock.

The theory behind tape-watching is that a new surge in buying may signal the start of a substantial rise in a given stock. Conversely, a lot of selling showing up on the tape could be a warning of a big decline ahead.

Not every investor has the time to watch the tape all day. So, to provide important daily trading data, *Investor's Business Daily* publishes the New York Stock Exchange Ticker Tape Study and the American Stock Exchange Ticker Tape Study.

Because of the time needed to sort the data, the ticker tape studies run a day behind. But this doesn't negate the usefulness of the data, which can help spot new investment ideas and trends.

Ticker Tape Box

Let's take a look at the Ticker Tape box.

The stocks are listed in two groups: those with the most on-balance up-tick volume and those with the largest on-balance down-tick volume.

NYSE
Ticker Tape Study For Monday

Company	Most Net Tic Volume	Close Price	Price Change
Blockbuster Entmt Corp	+ 795,900	17	+ ¾
Wells Fargo & Company	+ 708,000	72⅜	− 1⅜
Adams Express Co	+ 491,600	21	+ ⅜
A M P Inc	+ 457,500	57	− 7⅞
Consolidated Edison N Y	+ 419,200	31⅛	+ ⅛
Mcdonalds Corp	+ 411,800	47¼	+ ⅞
First Finl Mgmt Corp	+ 308,800	37⅞	+ 1¼
Oakwood Homes Corp	+ 294,800	17	− ¾
General Motors Corp Cl E	+ 282,300	29⅛	+ ⅛
Mattel Inc	+ 263,100	25⅜	+ ⅛
American Tel & Tel	+ 253,700	46⅝	+ 1
Chemical Waste Mgmt Inc	+ 244,000	21⅜	+ ⅛
Pfizer Inc	+ 242,100	76½	+ ½
Chemical Banking Corp	+ 240,700	36½	− ⅛
Advanced Micro Devices	+ 221,100	16⅜	− ⅛
Union Texas Pete Hldgs	− 969,000	17¾	− ⅝
Boston Scientific Corp	− 811,600	19	− ⅝
Humana Inc	− 657,700	19½	− ⅜
Union Electric Co	− 468,700	36⅛	......
Aluminum Co Of America	− 369,800	64⅝	− 1⅞
Moore Corp Ltd	− 361,000	15	− ½
Digital Equipment	− 342,800	33¾	− ⅜
Citicorp	− 299,900	17⅞	− ⅜
York Intl Corp	− 285,500	30½	− ½
Wellman Inc	− 279,900	19¼	+ ⅜
Schlumberger Ltd	− 276,900	60⅛	− ⅜
Long Island Lighting Co	− 248,000	24⅞	......
Toys R Us	− 245,600	36	− ⅜
U A L Corp	− 233,400	118¾	− 5⅛
Delta Air Lines Inc	− 232,500	53¼	− 3¾

A tick is the price change that takes place in a stock transaction. For example, if Wells Fargo & Co.'s last trade was 72 and the next trade was at 72 1/8, then it would be an "up tick." If the stock instead had fallen to 71 7/8, then it would have been a "down tick".

The total up-tick or down-tick volume is calculated for each stock traded on the exchanges by adding the total volume when the stock ticked up vs. the volume when it ticked down.

Stocks with the most up-tick volume for the day are listed in descending order for each exchange. Stocks with the most down-tick volume are shown in the bottom half of each table. Closing prices and price change are also included.

In the ticker study shown here, you can see that, of the NYSE issues, Blockbuster Entertainment Corp. had by far the most up-tick volume—795,900 shares—and closed up at 17. Likewise, Union Texas Petroleum Holdings Inc. had the most down-tick volume—969,000 shares—and closed down 5/8 at 17 3/4.

But remember: The ticker tape data should not be used by itself in choosing stocks to buy and sell. It is one of only several tools. Investors also need to be aware of company fundamentals and the technical position of the stock prices.

There are "tape traps", for example, which occur when investors blunder and buy an essentially flawed stock. It's up to the investor to sort out the smart buying and selling and not blindly follow the tape.

In another capacity, the ticker tape can be used to get a "feel" for the overall market. A rally may be nearing its end, for instance, when lower quality stocks—those with poor earnings and that have been lagging the market—start dominating the up-tick volume list.

On the other hand, the names that pop up on the up-tick list during the first stage of a major advance may turn out to be the market leaders. These stocks may also represent the vanguard of a rally for an entire industry.

World Stock Markets

Global Perspective At A Glance

■ **What's important is how a market is performing relative to other markets now.**

Today's well-informed investor has to watch not only the U.S. stock market, but the increasingly popular foreign markets as well. Many investors willing to venture abroad via a stock or mutual fund investment have done well in recent years.

As in the U.S., overseas markets have their leaders and laggards. Separating the two requires quite a bit of research and knowledge not only about the company you want to invest in, but also about the economic conditions in the country or countries in which it operates.

To keep investors in tune with world stock markets, *Investor's Business Daily* publishes every day a number of charts showing the price trends of markets around the world.

The charts and accompanying data cover 12 foreign markets including Japan, Mexico, Canada, Britain, Australia, Hong Kong, Germany and France, among others. The charts show weekly index changes and the percentage of increase or decrease over the past 12 months.

"More Global-Conscious"

"There is no doubt investors are becoming more global-conscious," said David Marvin of Marvin & Palmer Associates Inc., a Wilmington, Del., money management firm.

"There are two important variables to consider when investing overseas: first, the country's stock market and secondly, the value of its currency."

The world stock market charts shown in *Investor's Business*

Daily are in local currency. So an American investor must read-just the return from the value of the foreign currency to the U.S. dollar.

The index given in the *Investor's Business Daily* charts is called the capital international index and is based on 1970 being 100.

The index for the USA at that time was 400.9, indicating that the U.S. market had quadrupled since 1970. But that paled in comparison with the emerging Hong Kong market, which had made a 4,236% move.

What's most important, of course, is not what a market has done over the last two decades but how it's performing relative to other markets now. *Investor's Business Daily's* charts are especially helpful in this regard.

Note, for example, the U.S.—despite all the handwringing about its supposed lack of competitiveness—had the one stock market that didn't break down in 1992. It was also the first to move back into new-high ground. Not everyone, it seems, bought the conventional wisdom that America was not the place to be.

Investor's Business Daily also lists—under the heading "International Markets"—closing prices of some of the more widely-followed foreign securities.

A foreign security or mutual fund sometimes can be bought in the U.S. market under what is called an American Depositary Receipt. Stocks such as Sony Corp., Hitachi Ltd. and Reuters Ltd., and mutual funds such as the Germany Fund, the Korea Fund Inc. and the Taiwan Fund, can be purchased in this way.

Other issues will have to be purchased from markets overseas. Most major U.S. brokerage firms can handle the transaction. Many of the top U.S. brokers also provide research on many of the better-known overseas companies.

Psychological Market Indicators

Bearish/Bullish Sentiment

Going Against The Conventional Wisdom

■ **Investment advisory firms, taken as a group, are wrong most of the time.**

To fundamental and technical analysis, add psychological analysis to the tools that many successful investors use to stay ahead of the game.

A variety of indicators help them assess the mood of investors, and most of them appear in the "Psychological Market Indicators" box on *Investor's Business Daily's* General Market Indicators page.

The first indicator listed there is the percentage of investment advisors who are bearish or bullish.

Investors' Survey

The figure is derived by Investors Intelligence, a New Rochelle, N.Y.-based advisory service that publishes a newsletter that surveys 130 advisory firms that put out market letters. All are non-brokerage firms.

The survey was started in 1963. Since then, says editor Michael Burke, who has been with Investor's Intelligence since the start, the number of advisory firms has risen substantially, though quite a few went under in the bear market of 1973.

At first, it was thought that the advisory services would pick market tops and bottoms quite well. But to the surprise of some, including Burke and the rest of the Investors Intelligence staff, it turned out to be just the opposite.

They found that investment advisory firms, taken as a group, are wrong most of the time mainly because they are trend-followers.

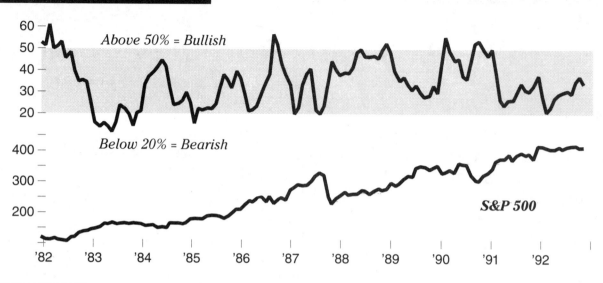

Bearish Advisors

Above 50% = Bullish

Below 20% = Bearish

S&P 500

'82 '83 '84 '85 '86 '87 '88 '89 '90 '91 '92

So, a contrary theory prevailed—that is, when most investment advisers are bullish and few are bearish, the stock market is close to a top. And when many advisers are bearish and only a few bullish, the market is near a bottom.

There is a lead time. Generally, peaks in bullishness or bearishness among the advisers come before the market actually tops or bottoms, rather than being coincidental.

In bull markets, moreover, corrections end quickly and tops take longer. In bear markets, bottoms take longer to develop.

Market Drop

According to Burke, when the number of bullish advisory firms climbs to more than 54% and bears dip below 20%, it's time to expect a drop in the market.

When the stock market is in a corrective phase, Burke says, investors should look for the bullish advisory firms to go below 40% and the bears to increase to 30% or more. At that point, a

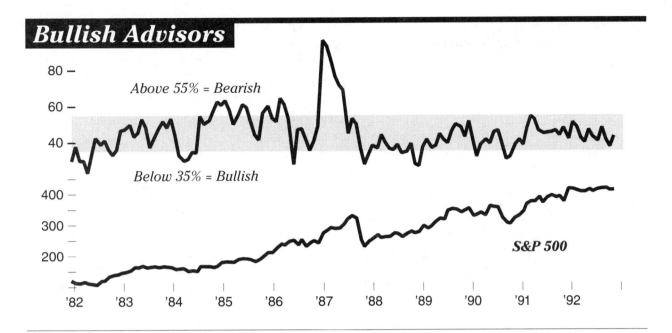

Bullish Advisors

Above 55% = Bearish

Below 35% = Bullish

S&P 500

'82 '83 '84 '85 '86 '87 '88 '89 '90 '91 '92

rally can be expected.

In a bear market—when the Dow drops 15% or more—the percentage of bearish advisors needs to climb to 55% or 60% before a bottom is reached and an upturn can be expected.

When the market was bottoming in 1982, Burke notes, his indicator was 62% bearish. The final low was made that August. The Dow then surged several hundred points before a majority of the advisory services became bullish, he recalled.

Contrarian Indicator

Harry Laubscher, stock market analyst at Tucker, Anthony & R.L. Day Inc. in New York, has found Investors Intelligence's sentiment reading a very helpful contrarian indicator when considered with other market indexes.

"I know that historically it seems to have worked well, but not always," Laubscher says. "It performs very well on the bearish side during a bull market.

"If the market's trend is positive, and there is a large bearish reading, it's usually a good time to buy. In a bearish market, a large number of bearish advisors is sometimes accurate for a bottom."

Odd-Lot Short Sales

Tracking The Wrong-Way Crowd

■ **The crowd is usually wrong when it comes to picking the direction of the market.**

"Like lemmings rushing to the sea, cycle after cycle, the odd-lot short sellers (individuals that short less than 100 shares at a time) appear to be a group hellbent on self-destruction," said Norman Fosback, who heads the Institute for Econometric Research in Fort Lauderdale, Fla.

The ratio of odd-lot short sellers to odd-lot sales is one of the psychological market indicators that appears each day in *Investor's Business Daily*.

The general interpretation is that the higher the ratio—meaning more short selling by odd lotters—the more bullish the outlook for the market. That's because odd lotters are almost always wrong.

Technical analysts who pay attention to odd-lot short selling use it in conjunction with other sentiment indicators, such as put-to-call ratios.

Many analysts still consider the odd lot short selling indicator to be one of the best barometers of "crowd psychology." The crowd is usually wrong when it comes to picking the direction of the market, therefore the index is an excellent contrarian indicator.

But despite the index's record, some analysts say it's getting to be less effective. "It was a phenomenal indicator 20 years ago until everyone started to following it," said one technician.

"Short selling offers an extremely poor reward-risk relationship," Fosback said.

"Anyone who engages in short selling must either be remark-

Odd-Lot Short Sales

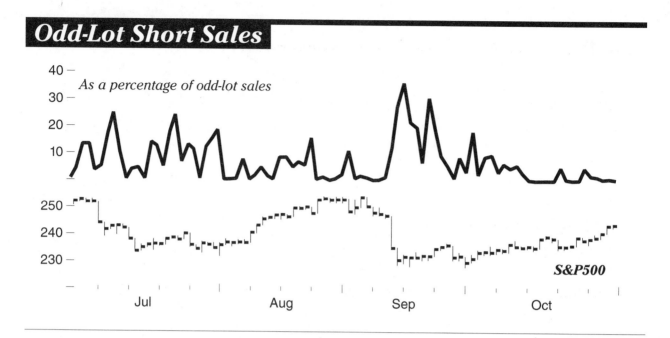

As a percentage of odd-lot sales

S&P500

ably intelligent to profit from it or incredibly naive to try," Fosback continued. "The odd-lotter short seller falls into the latter class."

As a group, odd-lot short sellers are traders who, because of their limited funds, must deal in small amounts of stock.

Fosback's research revealed when the odd-lot short sale index on a 10-week moving average basis climbs above 4.0, the probability for rising stock prices is 100% and the average gain after a year 23.4%.

When the indicator was under 0.5, indicating less shorting, Fosback found the probability of rising stock prices was more than 30% and a year later the average gain was 6.2%.

When many stocks are selling at low prices after a market decline and the odd-lot short selling continues to be strong, the odd-lot short selling index is even more bullish.

Public/NYSE Specialist Short Sales

Keeping An Eye On The Smart Money

■ **Short selling by NYSE specialists is considered by many to be a fairly good indicator of future stock-market trends.**

The ability to call stock-market turns is what separates the experts from the also-rans.

Short selling by NYSE specialists is considered by many to be a fairly good indicator of future stock-market trends.

A short sale is the sale of a borrowed security. The seller must eventually buy and return the borrowed security. That's known as short covering.

A specialist is a member of the exchange. His or her job is to maintain an orderly market in selected securities. In fulfilling this function, specialists act as brokers in opening the market and executing orders.

They also buy and sell for their own accounts to provide market depth and price continuity in their specialty stock. Weekly trading activity of specialists is available to the public by the Securities and Exchange Commission.

Specialist Activity

Market researchers have found specialists quite accurate in their short sales. In order to help readers track specialist activity, *Investor's Business Daily* keeps track of NYSE specialist short-selling in the "Psychological Market Indicators" box on the General Market Indicators page.

Studies show that when the ratio is high—above 0.6, meaning the specialists have not undertaken many short sales—the market is likely to move higher. Conversely, when specialists do have large short positions shown by a ratio of 0.35 or below—

Public/NYSE Specialst Short Sales

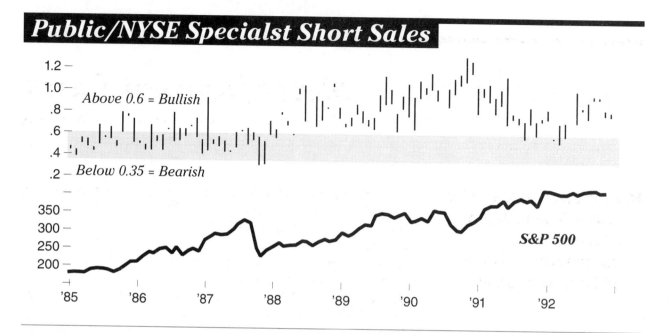

the market generally moves lower.

Although the index provides clues, it's not infallible.

Before the 1987 crash, the ratio was around 0.5, giving no hint a big market plunge was coming. There have also been times when specialists used options to set up their positions. So, investors have to be careful when using the index.

Heavy shorting by specialists, moreover, can result from an overpowering rally in the market that places huge demands on their market-making capacity, and which they fulfill by supplying stock short.

The ratio has been helpful at some junctures, however.

The chart above, for example, show the ratio spiking in early 1987, as a major runup in advance of the crash was building steam; in the fall of 1988, at the beginning of a 10-month, 33% move in the Dow industrial average, and again in the fall of 1990, when a three-month bear market was ending and a new bull market was getting under way.

Short Interest Ratio

Still Another Gauge Of Market Fuel Levels

■ **Stock borrowed to be sold will eventually have to be purchased, and that will create demand.**

In stock-market investing, there are bulls, who buy a stock hoping it'll go up, and bears, who sell the stock outright or sell it "short," believing it is headed lower.

A "short sale" occurs when an investor sells stock he doesn't own. He borrows the stock certificates from a broker in order to make delivery to the buyer.

It's the opposite of buying first and selling later. He sells first and buys back later.

If the stock price falls, the investor buys it back at the lower price and repays the debt to the brokerage. In the process, he pockets the difference between the higher selling price and the lower buyback price.

Short-selling is not new. Jacob Little, one of the first great stock market operators, used short-selling in the 1800s. Later, such famous names as Vanderbilt, Drew, Fisk and Gould employed the practice.

Until 1929, there were no accurate statistics on short sales. Three weeks following the crash in October of that year, the New York Stock Exchange gathered the first figures on short "interest."

SEC Regulation

Since then, the Securities and Exchange Commission has established rules on short sales. Also, the NYSE, the American Stock Exchange and the National Association of Securities Dealers, which oversees the Nasdaq, now publish monthly figures on short sales.

The information is published around the 15th of each month in *Investor's Business Daily* and a few other newspapers. The data show total short interest outstanding and the short interest on each stock.

How can an investors use these numbers?

The basic principle is that large short interest is usually bullish for the overall market and for an individual stock. The idea is that stock borrowed to be sold will eventually have to be purchased, and that will increase demand for the stock and push the price higher.

But shorts won't purchase the stock in significant quantity until the stock starts to move higher on its own. If such as "squeeze" develops, many shorts will be forced to buy the stock, or "cover" their positions, before it moves even higher and their losses mount.

Categories Of Short-Sellers

Short-sellers are divided into four types:

- Speculators, who sell short in hopes of the stock market moving lower.
- Hedgers, who try to reduce their risk on long, or regular, positions.
- Arbitrageurs, who try to gain by shorting a stock and going long a related security, such as a convertible preferred or an option.
- NYSE specialists, who use short sales to maintain orderly markets.

When reporting short sales, *Investor's Business Daily* also notes the "short interest ratio." This the ratio of short interest to total market volume for the period. When the short interest ratio moves above 2.5%, it's a bullish sign for the market. Below 1.5% is bearish.

The actual amount of short interest reported by the exchanges and the Nasdaq alone is of little value. What matters is the ratio and its trend. *Investor's Business Daily* lists the short interest for the current and preceding month. This will tell you if short interest is increasing.

Importantly, the percentage of increase is also given. That way, you can scan the tables at a glance for any dramatic changes.

The *Investor's Business Daily* tables also show a stock's average daily volume for the period. By comparing this figure with the amount of short interest outstanding, an investor can also get a feel for how much impact a burst of short-covering might have on the stock's price.

As with most indicators, short interest should never be viewed in isolation. It's important to research the background of a company and study its chart pattern before making any decisions based solely on how much of its stock has been sold short.

Mutual Fund Buys, Redemptions

Still More Clues To Market Turns

■ **When fund purchases are high, the funds have additional cash to buy stocks, and the market moves higher.**

Of all the stock-market players, equity mutual funds are among the largest and most active.

For years, analysts have studied fund cash reserves and the flow of purchases and redemptions by shareholders to measure the potential stock buying power of the funds and to glean possible trends in the stock market.

To help readers stay on top of fund activity, *Investor's Business Daily* publishes in its "Psychological Market Indicators" box the ratio of mutual fund share purchases vs. redemptions, excluding money market funds.

The theory is that when fund purchases are high—thus making the ratios high—the funds will have additional cash to buy stocks. Therefore, the market should move higher.

Conversely, when the ratio of fund purchases to redemptions is low—hinting of a probable drain of cash—the market will face slower going because the funds won't have cash to buy stocks and in fact may have to sell shares to pay for redemptions.

Bull Markets

The strategy worked like a charm during the bull market of the 1980s. For example, the ratio of fund purchases to redemptions hit one of its highest levels on Oct. 1, 1985, when it stood at 4.63. From there, the Dow Jones industrial average soared from 1350 to 1900 in 11 months—a gain of 41%.

After the market consolidated for a few months, the ratio of fund purchases to redemptions index stood at 3.11 on Nov. 28, and the Dow again broke out from a base at 1900 to soar to 2700, another 42% advance.

Not surprisingly, the ratio fell to one of its lowest levels in the crash of October 1987, which triggered a stampede of redemptions by many fund shareholders.

With the ratio so low at that point, few expected the stock market to move up very much for a while. But an astute market watcher would have kept close tabs on the ratio, watching for signs of improvement.

In mid-November 1992, the ratio was 2.03, a little more than halfway between its five-year high and low.

A recent high of 2.48 was set July 31, 1992, five weeks after *Investor's Business Daily's* Mutual Fund Index of 20 diversified growth funds bottomed and just before it entered a 3-week correction.

New Trends

Interestingly, mutual fund managers and the stock market in general may have been helped in the past year or two by a growing tendency among investors not to redeem shares in equity funds when the market corrects.

For example, many growth fund managers said they were able to weather the abortive Soviet coup in 1991 with their portfolios intact. Whatever redemptions occurred weren't extensive enough to force them to sell positions in order to return shareholders' money.

As mutual funds continue to become the preferred vehicle for long-term retirement plans, more and more fund investors may be content to let their investments ride out market corrections.

The bigger the slice of the market that mutual funds control, the greater the implication this phenomenom may have for the market's ability to withstand panics sparked by news events.

The share purchases vs. redemptions ratio can also be used as a contrarian indicator during a bear market. When fund redemptions are at their height in a market slump, investor psychology tends to be completely negative.

Though few investors can muster the courage to buy when everything looks so terrible, that is the very time the long-term investor should be purchasing most aggressively.

OTC Vs. NYSE Trading Volume

A Reliable Measure Of Frothiness

■ **Speculation increases OTC volume, and this can predict major turns in the market.**

Speculation in stocks, as in other things, is best done in moderation.

When speculation is running high, it usually signals that the stock market is approaching a top. Conversely, when speculation is low, a market bottom may be at hand.

But how do you know when speculation, or the lack of it, has gone to extremes?

One of the best ways is to compare trading in the Over-The-Counter market to that on the New York Stock Exchange. The ratio of OTC to NYSE volume is published in *Investor's Business Daily* in the "Psychological Market Indicators" box on the General Market Indicators page.

As the chart on the next page shows, spikes in the OTC-NYSE ratio have coincided with several market tops over the past ten years. January of 1992 was one recent example.

Other notable spikes occurred in mid-1983 (which turned out to be a major top in small-capitalization issues), in mid-1987 (in advance of the October collapse) and in the spring of 1990 (just before that year's bear market set in).

The ratio fell to abnormally low levels in July 1982 (the eve of the super bull market) and in the fall of 1990 (the end of that year's bear phase).

Secondary Issues

A high ratio reflects increased trading in secondary issues. The Nasdaq market is considered a benchmark for speculative

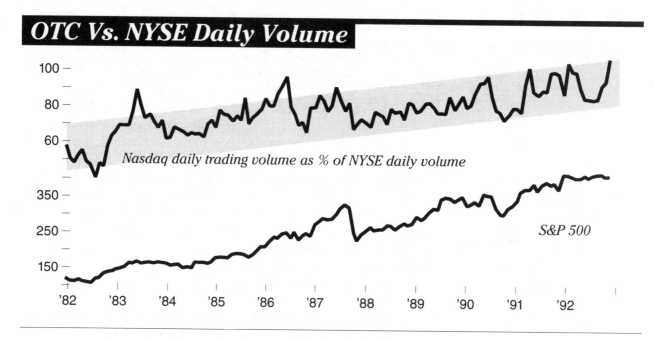

OTC Vs. NYSE Daily Volume

Nasdaq daily trading volume as % of NYSE daily volume

S&P 500

activity because it is bursting with emerging small- and mid-cap growth stocks favored by many individual investors. Most new issues also trade on the Nasdaq.

Contrary Indicator

The ratio is considered a "contrary" indicator because investors should be getting more cautious, not less, as trading becomes more speculative.

The more bullish investors become, the more money they invest. But as more money is invested, less is available for the further buying required to push the market even higher, explains Richard Freeman, portfolio manager of the SLB Aggressive Growth fund and executive vice president of Shearson Asset Management in New York.

Thus, charting the OTC-NYSE volume ratio can be a handy tool for determining major market turns.

Market Tops

Merely noting when the ratio climbs above 100—showing that OTC trading has exceeded that on the NYSE—can be helpful.

Claudia Mott, director of small-cap research at Prudential Securities Inc., has found that a soaring Nasdaq accompanied by volume that overwhelms the Big Board's is a reliable sign of a market top.

Mott explained that watchers of this phenomenon "feel that speculative institutional buying, which tends to chase rallies in any market, leads to an increase in volume. This speculative frenzy eventually pushes the Nasdaq market to technical extremes and a correction results.

"Another school," she adds, "feels that the volume increase is a result of individuals getting into the market late in the cycle and creating much of the same effect."

The first time OTC volume exceeded the Big Board's was in 1983. And that, Mott noted, preceded a slump in small-cap stocks that lasted until 1985. The ratio of OTC to NYSE volume has been expanding for the past ten years as the OTC market has grown. Many companies, such as Microsoft Corp. and Amgen Inc., which may have left for the Big Board long ago are staying on the Nasdaq system. Also, the Nasdaq is attracting a huge number of IPOs.

Years ago, the Microsofts and the Amgens, once established, would have fled to the Big Board in search of greater liquidity. But that's no longer a problem, said Freeman.

Stock Splits

Not necessarily good news

■ **A high number of splits indicates the entire market may be nearing a top.**

Keeping track of stock splits can help investors gauge both the future performance of individual stocks and the market as a whole.

A large number of splits, either in a given stock or the market as a whole, is an indication that prices have moved significantly higher and may be reaching a top.

The logic is pretty simple and often boils down to a matter of supply and demand.

If XYZ Corp. splits its stock 2-for-1, shareholders end up with twice as many shares valued at half the price. In other words, if a company has 2 million shares valued at $100 apiece, a 2-for-1 will result in four million shares priced at $50. Split it 3-for-1 and there will be six million shares valued at $33.33 each.

A powerful stock can easily withstand several splits over the course of several years. But if the trend continues and intensifies, the new supply of stock may begin to outstrip demand, especially if earnings begin to slow.

That's why a stock can more easily withstand a 2-for-1 split than a 4-for-1, because the supply is merely doubled rather than quadrupled.

Attracting Investors

In most cases, companies split their stocks only after they have moved significantly higher. The idea is to lower the price to make them more attractive to individual investors.

It stands to reason, then, that if a stock has undergone several splits within a relatively short period—say 18 months—it has moved rapidly higher and may have reached the end of its most spectacular capital appreciation.

The same idea can be applied to the market as a whole. A high number of splits indicates that the entire market may be nearing a top.

Investor's Business Daily lists the number of stock splits each day in the Psychological Market Indicators section on the General Market Indicators page.

Forthcoming Market Collapse

In June 1987—four months before the market collapse—the number of splits in the *Investor's Business Daily* 6,000-stock index hit a peak of 169. In other words, 169 stocks had split during the previous 30 days.

Watching splits is hardly foolproof, however. The indicator reached a five-year peak of 127 stocks on June 16, 1992. The market went sideways for the next several months, then rallied in October.

In that case, investors started bidding up stocks as an improving economy gave rise to expectations for better corporate profits. Both the market and individual stocks can weather a lot of splits as long as underlying fundamentals corporate earnings, inflation and interest rates remain favorable.

Conversely, a low number of splits can help identify market bottoms. For instance, on Nov. 26, 1990, just as the market was embarking on a major bull phase, the number of splits sank to a five-year low of 20. The reasoning: stock prices were already low and any attempt to split them would trim their prices too much.

New-Issue Activity

Another Sign Of Approaching Tops And Bottoms

■ **A hot new-issue market usually accompanies a more speculative environment and often signals a market top.**

Of the many psychological indicators that help give investors a feel for where the market is in its cycle, new-issue activity is one of the best.

A sluggish new-issue market is often a sign that a bear market is over or that stocks are about to move higher. New-issue activity is viewed as a contrarian indicator. When interest in new issues has been low, the market has frequently moved higher.

"When you've got a moribund new-issue market coupled with historically low relative valuations and relatively negative investor psychology, there's great potential for the market," said Dan Case, head of investment banking for Hambrecht & Quist Inc. in San Francisco.

Signaling A Market Top

Conversely, a hot new-issue market usually accompanies a more speculative environment and often signals a market top.

A quick way of sizing up activity in new issues is by comparing their number over the past year to the number of stocks traded on the New York Stock Exchange. The resulting ratio is a measure of the relative supply of new issues.

This ratio is updated and published each day in *Investor's Business Daily* as one of its "Psychological Market Indicators."

Glenn S. Cutler, a newsletter publisher, uses the ratio to gauge "the level of speculation in the market."

One of the highest points the new-issue index reached over the last several years was 49.5% in March of 1987, five months before the major top in August and seven months before the crash, Cutler noted.

Similarly, he said, the low made in October 1988 came shortly before a rally that eventually carried the S&P 500 index up 36% in 11 months.

Economic Growth

Analysts cite two reasons why initial offerings tend to increase as the market moves higher. First, rising markets generally occur during periods of economic growth when privately held firms need more capital for expansion and research.

Second, a bull market encourages owners of privately held concerns to take their companies public so they can sell a portion of the firm at considerable profit and still remain in control.

The new-issue ratio declines with the market for the opposite reasons. The economy is stagnant when stock prices are low, and private companies don't need as much capital. And they don't want to sell their stock to the public at low valuations.

Market Bottom

It's just at these market points, when the index is low, that a market bottom may be at hand.

In the early 1980s, the index hit a low of 5.5% in January 1983, when the Dow Jones industrial average was around 950. At that point, the Dow had just moved up 150 points in five months. But the index was saying more was to come, and indeed it eventually moved higher.

The ratio was abnormally high—35.7% on Nov. 17, 1987—just after the crash. This may have reflected a large number of companies that had committed to come public during the strong market runup earlier in the year.

A recent low was 9.2%, on May 2, 1991, when a market correction was nearing completion.

Dow Indicators

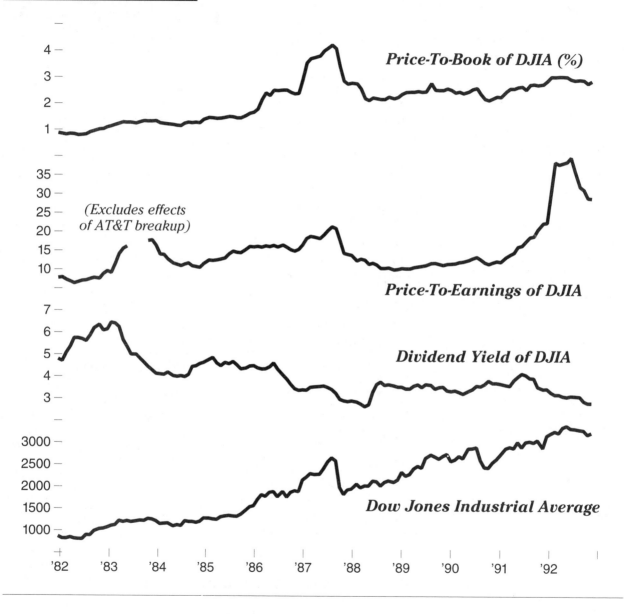

Price-To-Book of DJIA (%)

(Excludes effects of AT&T breakup)

Price-To-Earnings of DJIA

Dividend Yield of DJIA

Dow Jones Industrial Average

'82 '83 '84 '85 '86 '87 '88 '89 '90 '91 '92

Valuing The Dow

Indicators Used By Value Players Warned Of Market Plunge Ahead

■ **Price-to-book, price-to-earnings, and dividend yield ratios can help determine if the market is fairly valued.**

Among the many approaches to analyzing the outlook for the stock market are those most popular with "value players." They typically involve a study of various corporate productivity measures such as dividends, earnings and book value.

Included among the "Psychological Market Indicators" appearing each day in *Investor's Business Daily* are three of the yardsticks most often used to determine if the market is over-valued, undervalued or fairly valued. They are:

   ■ The price-to-book value of the Dow Jones industrial average.
   ■ The price-to-earnings ratio of the Dow.
   ■ The dividend yield of the Dow.

Price-To-Book

The price-to-book value of the Dow is found by taking the sum of the assets minus the liabilities of all stocks making up the blue-chip index. The figure, called net worth, is divided by the shares outstanding to derive the book value, which is then compared to the combined prices of the Dow stocks.

The book value does have a degree of inaccuracy in that it does not always reflect the true net worth of a firm because of various methods of accounting. However, the figure used in *Investor's Business Daily* is the best possible and serves the purpose well.

When the price-to-book value is low, the market could be considered undervalued; when it is high, it may be viewed as overvalued. The price-to-book reached one of its highest points—4.50—in June 1987, when the Dow was around 2300—four months and 400 points before the big October plunge from 2700. One of its lowest levels was 1.06 in January 1983, when Dow was 1050 and in the middle of the first leg of the '80s bull market.

P-E Ratio

The price-to-earnings ratio of the Dow is calculated by dividing the current price of the stocks into the earnings for the past 12 months. The Dow P-E found in *Investor's Business Daily* sometimes differs from that calculated by other newspapers because of the way earnings are figured.

Investor's Business Daily, for example, does not include one-time items in calculating earnings. It is interested only in the profitability of a company's ongoing operations.

With so many members of the Dow Jones industrial average undergoing major restructurings, exclusion of extraordinary items sometimes creates major discrepancies between the Dow multiple shown in IBD and that shown elsewhere.

When the P-E ratio is high, the market is considered pricey. If it's low, the market is considered undervalued. Many "value" money managers will not buy stocks if P-Es are above certain levels. This in itself can put a damper on the market.

Value players complained at various points during the 1980s that they had a hard time finding low P-E stocks. And rightly so. The P-E for the Dow hit an abnormally high 22.1 in August 1987—probably the clearest warning of a market top.

Dividend Yield

The last of the "value indicators" is the dividend yield of the Dow. This also flashed a yellow light to investors prior to the October 1987 crash. The yield on the Dow slipped to a five-year low of 2.58% in late August, five weeks before the big drop.

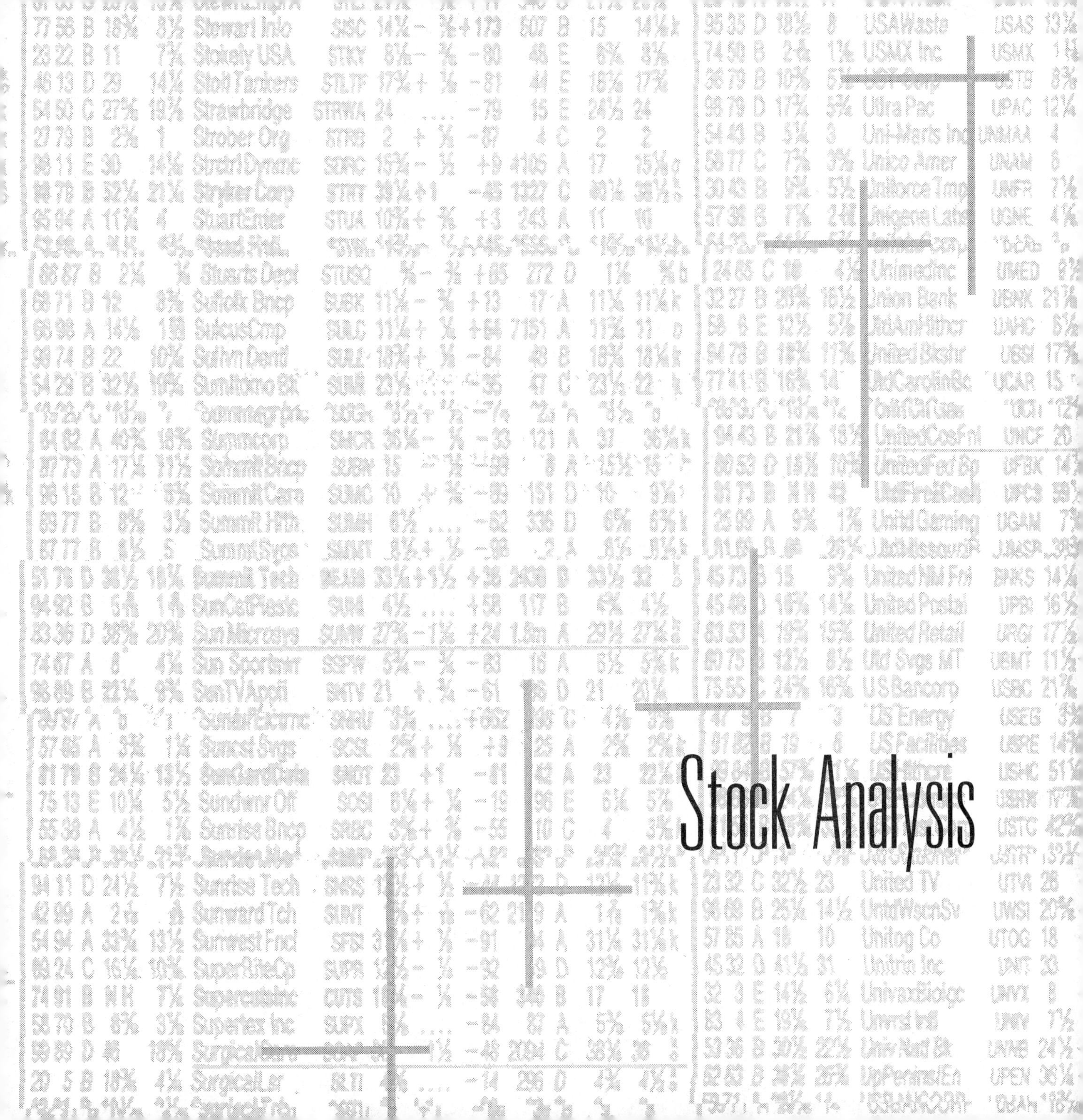

Stock Analysis

Earnings Per Share Rank

Profitability At A Glance

■ **Stocks that do best are those companies whose earnings are growing fast.**

Investor's Business Daily has a lot of numbers, but none may be as important for stock investors as the one under the heading "Earnings Per Share rank."

The EPS rank comes first in every stock listing for good reason. It encapsulates what may be the most important thing the investor needs to know about the thousands of investment opportunities available to him—the company's profitability.

A study by William O'Neil & Co., a sister company of Investor's Business Daily Inc., of the greatest stocks of the last 40 years found that strong earnings growth is what most of them had in common. This one characteristic far outweighed others that are often used to judge stocks, such as price-earnings ratios and dividend yields.

More specifically, the study found the most successful stocks were those of companies that coupled powerful earnings gains in recent quarters with solid five-year records of profitable operations.

Yet, until *Investor's Business Daily* came along, investors had no way of telling—at least from their newspaper—how profitable a company was.

EPS Rank

To fill this void, and to help readers readily see which companies are the most successful, *Investor's Business Daily* came up with EPS rank, a valuable fundamental measurement that lets you compare profit growth of one company with all others.

SynOptics Communications Inc.

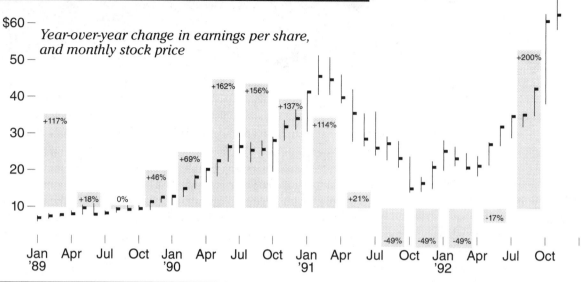

Year-over-year change in earnings per share, and monthly stock price

EPS measures a company's earnings growth over the last five years and the stability of that growth. Then, the percentage change in the last two quarters' earnings vs. the same quarters a year earlier is combined and averaged with the five-year figure.

The result is compared to *all* companies in *Investor's Business Daily's* stock tables (*not*, as some people think, to other stocks on the same exchange or stocks in the same industry group) and ranked on a scale of 1 to 99.

An EPS rank of 90 means the company produced earnings results in the top 10%. Companies with superior earnings records have EPS ranks of 80 or higher.

Stock Performance

If you get a longer-term chart book, you will see that the stocks that did best were those of companies whose earnings were growing fast. In fact, the more explosive the profit growth, the sharper the stock-price gains. Similarly, when earnings faltered, so did the stocks.

The SynOptics chart, for example, shows how the stock took off and then gained momentum as earnings growth accelerated in late 1989 and into 1990. It continued to climb as SynOptics continued to post double-digit profit gains (its EPS in this period was 99—the highest possible).

But the stock topped as growth decelerated in the first half of '91, and fell sharply as the company started to report negative results. As growth reaccelerated in '92, the stock recovered to new highs.

Because it is calculated with reported earnings, EPS rank will not signal profit slowdowns up the road. The stock action—as measured by the Relative Strength rank—will generally do that.

In SynOptics case, the Relative Strength line, after two years of making higher highs and higher lows, started making lower highs and lower lows early in the second quarter of 1991 just after the stock topped and before it fell another 50%.

Relative Strength

Winnowing The Wheat From The Chaff

■ **Most great stocks have high Relative Strength ranks *before* their major price moves.**

Because stock selection is so important to good performance, investors need all the tools they can get their hands on to identify those issues with the best chance of success.

One of the best is Relative Strength—a way of measuring the performance of one stock or industry group to all others to see how strong or weak it is by comparison.

The idea is that if a stock or group is beginning to outperform, that should indicate future strength in the market and thus an opportunity to buy.

If the Relative Strength is falling, the stock or group is weakening and thus should be avoided or even shorted.

Investor's Business Daily uses Relative Strength extensively in its stock tables and charts and its industry group rankings.

Computing Relative Strength

The Relative Strength number that appears for each stock is calculated by comparing its price change over the past 12 months to that of all other stocks in the tables. Results are ranked 1 to 99.

An RS of 99 is the highest possible and means the stock has outperformed 99% of all stocks in the past 12 months. A rank of 1 means nearly all other issues have done better. Market leaders usually rank 80 or higher.

A study by William O'Neil & Co., a sister company of Investor's Business Daily Inc., of the great stocks of the last 40 years found an average RS of 87 *before* their major price moves began.

Don Hays, director of investment strategy at Wheat First Butcher & Singer Inc. in Richmond, Va., has done a lot of original work on Relative Strength.

"It's very important," he says. "But unfortunately, it is the hardest thing to sell to average investors because generally they like to 'bottom fish' (buy stocks down substantially in price in hopes they are near their lows). In most cases, they'll lose money going after down-and-out stocks."

Investor's Business Daily also plots a Relative Strength line for each of the dozens of stocks charted in the paper every day. The RS line is derived by dividing a stock's price by the close of the S&P 500 index.

Behavior of the line is often an early tipoff to a major move in a stock.

Major Moves

For example, the RS line of Home Depot moved sharply higher in May 1992 while the stock itself was still moving sideways. Eventually the stock followed the RS line into new-high ground, and to much higher levels from there.

The Relative Strength line can also signal potential trouble. Notice how Ballard Medical Products, a stock that already (from early 1989) had risen tenfold, climbed to yet-another new high in late March of 1992.

But notice also that its RS line stayed below its prior peak, failing to confirm the stock's breakout. The stock broke down thereafter. Lesson: If the RS line doesn't precede or confirm the stock's move, watch out.

Hays uses Relative Strength with earnings momentum to select stocks. "A stock can get into a buy zone even if it has a Relative Strength as low as 60," in his opinion, although earnings momentum in such cases must be very high.

"We weigh Relative Strength more heavily than earnings momentum," he explains. Even if the earnings aren't there yet, Hays would still buy the stock if it has a Relative

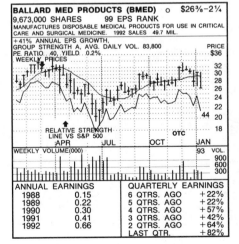

Strength of 90 or higher because the market is indicating the earnings will improve substantially.

"I think Relative Strength is better than earnings momentum in predicting future appreciation in a stock," he says.

Stocks with a Relative Strengths above 95 can be good trading plays for one to three months, he says. But one must be careful, he adds: If the market environment turns nasty, these issues are likely to be hit especially hard.

"Generally, we like to buy for the six- to 24-month period," says Hays. "After we buy our stocks, we follow the trend of the Relative Strength line by tabulating the stock's Relative Strength from day to day. What we want to see is a pattern of higher highs and higher lows. A divergence is a warning signal."

General Market Indicator

Hays also uses a Relative Strength measure to assess the overall market. He calls it the "blue chip-white chip index." It compares the S&P 500 index (blue chip) against the Value Line arithmetic average (white chip). (Both indexes appear in *Investor's Business Daily.*)

When blue chips dominate, Hays say, it means people want defensive stocks. When white chips start doing well, it means people are willing to go after growth stocks.

Accumulation-Distribution Rating

Getting Down To Specifics Of Supply And Demand

■ **When buying stocks breaking out of proper bases, make sure they have a rating of 'A' or 'B'.**

Knowing when there is more buying in a stock than selling, and vice versa, isn't easy.

Investor's Business Daily has a unique and important measure to simplify the task: a simple letter grade that's included in nearly every stock listing.

The accumulation-distribution (Acc.-Dis.) rating takes into account the percent change in a stock's daily price and its volume.

The ratings go from "A" to "E". An "A" or "B" rating means a stock has been showing accumulation. "C" is a neutral rating, and a "D" or "E" means a stock has been under distribution.

There are two proprietary adjustments. The daily A-E value is adjusted for the percent change in the close relative to the stock's daily trading range. Also, any unusual spikes in volume caused by offerings or other irregular circumstances are eliminated to smooth the data and avoid distortions.

Basic Principles

The basic principle is that accumulation takes place when a stock trades on heavy volume and its price rises at the same time, or when it trades on heavy volume and closes at the high end of its daily trading range. The same principle applies when using weekly bar charts.

The market action is saying there is plenty of demand for the stock and the probability is that the price will move higher.

Distribution occurs in just the opposite way. A stock will trade big volume but drop in price, or close at the lower end of its daily range. In some cases, there will be heavy volume and no upward progress in price. That's called "churning" and is also a form of distribution.

Market Clues

When distribution is taking place, the market is saying the supply of stock for sale is outstripping demand. It's a prelude to an eventual drop in price, which may come days or even weeks later.

The idea of correlating price and volume is not new. Joseph Granville came up with his indicator called "on-balance volume." Marc Chaikin, a partner at Bomar Securities Inc., tried to improve on it with his Chaikin Oscillator, and futures trader James Sibbet developed a very complicated indicator called the Demand Index.

Investor's Business Daily's accumulation-distribution rating is not a stand-alone buy or sell signal. It is one of several tools an investor should use when making an investment decision.

Dennis Jarrett, market analyst at Kidder, Peabody & Co., uses an accumulation and distribution indicator that he calls "money flow." He makes his investment decisions based on that and at least four other indicators used to improve his stock selection.

Guidelines

Here are some guidelines in using *Investor's Business Daily's* accumulation-distribution ratings:

- When buying stocks breaking out of proper bases, make sure they have an accumulation-distribution rating of "A" or "B".
- Buying a stock with an "A" or "B" rating still in a base or pulling back after an up move is a bit premature but can work. Jarrett favors this technique.

- Be wary when a stock you're holding drops to a "D" or "E" rating. It may be time to sell, even though the stock's price has yet to show any deterioration. Remember that distribution will precede a decline in price.
- After a move up, a stock that goes into a basing formation should maintain a rating of at least a "C".
- If the leaders in an industry group show a falloff to a "C," "D" or "E" rating, keep a close eye on other stocks in the group.
- If many leading stocks in the market drop to "C," "D" or "E" ratings, the overall market will have trouble advancing.

Volume Percent Change

Often An Early Sign Of The Start Of Something Big

■ **Volume is the closest thing to "the ultimate technical tool."**

In the spring of 1992, Scientific Atlanta Inc. looked like just another $16 stock on a slow train to nowhere.

Sales and earnings for the manufacturer of telecommunications equipment seemed to be rebounding after two long years of miserable results. But its share price, when it moved at all, seldom ticked up or down more than an eighth or quarter-point. Its average volume on the New York Stock Exchange was a torpid 30,000 shares a day.

Then, in the first week of May, Scientific Atlanta started acting funny. There were sessions when it traded more than twice its average volume, and when the shares ticked up as much as 3/4.

On May 11, the stock leaped 1 3/4 points to 18 1/2 on volume of 470,000 shares—more than 15 times normal.

So began a move that made Scientific Atlanta one of the best-performing stocks in the entire market. In seven months, it had doubled on an explosion of volume that on some days topped 570,000 shares. By Thanksgiving, its average daily turnover had swollen to 167,000 shares.

Abnormal Volume

The Scientific Atlanta example—one of hundreds crossing the tape every day—points out how important a stock's trading activity is, and how abnormal volume can often signal major moves—both up and down—in a stock before it's obvious to others.

None of this, of course, is news to market analysts or professional investors. Volume—in individual stocks or the general market—is one of their most important tools.

Individual investors have long been at a disadvantage when it came to using volume as a technical tool. But with the advent of personal computer programs that track trading activity, and especially with redesigned newspaper stock tables such as those pioneered by *Investor's Business Daily*, this has changed significantly.

The Best Tool

Volume is the closest thing to "the ultimate technical tool," according to Mark Leibovit, formerly a market analyst for a Chicago securities firm and now a newsletter publisher in Arizona.

Noting the oft-heard axiom that "volume precedes price," Leibovit believes that trend changes are more often than not signaled by significant changes in relative volume that is, trading that is higher than normal.

When a stock moves up on heavier-than-average volume, Leibovit says, "the general meaning is that it's being purchased by the so-called 'smart money,' or that insiders are making a directed effort to buy it because they think it's going up."

The reverse is true, Leibovit adds, for stocks moving down on heavy volume.

In watching individual stocks, some basic price and volume principles should be kept in mind.

When the general market is trending higher, a stock rising on increasing volume is bullish. A stock rising on lower volume, however, is suspect. Flat prices on heavy volume are also suspect and are viewed as a sign of "churning"—a situation in which selling of the stock is just a heavy as the buying. A stock falling on heavy volume, especially in an up market, is bearish and often a sign of bad news to come.

In a weak market, a declining price accompanied by heavy volume is also bearish. But lower prices on extremely heavy volume could signal a bottom in a stock. This situation is referred to as a climactic sell-off in which selling is quickly exhausted. Lower prices accompanied by a significant contraction of volume can be bullish because it could signal that selling is drying up or has been completed.

The accompanying chart on the price and volume action in Scientific Atlanta helps show how trading can be analyzed.

Scientific Atlanta

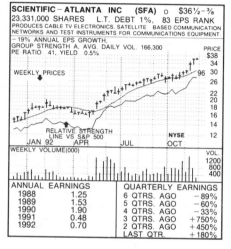

In December 1991 and early January 1992, the stock was working its way higher on generally increasing volume. Then it leveled off on low volume. In the first week of February, the stock rose with volume picking up again.

But in the second week of February, it was unable to make further progress even though volume remained relatively heavy. This churning action marked a top and the beginning of a three-month correction.

As the correction wore on, however, volume shriveled up—indicating that the selling was exhausting itself. Then came the May rally on heavy volume.

The same principles apply to the general market. It's bullish, for example, when the major indexes—such as the Dow Jones industrial average—move higher on increasing volume.

But if the indexes stall out on continued heavy volume, it's often a sign the market is topping.

The operative word in any discussion of volume is "relative." It isn't enough to know how many of a company's shares trade each day—a figure that appears in every newspaper. What's important is how that figure differs, if at all, from the stock's average daily turnover.

Investor's Business Daily stock tables not only list total volume for each stock each day but also show the percentage by which that volume varies from each stock's average over the prior 50 trading days. To make it even easier to spot unusual activity, volume percent changes of 50% or more are boldfaced.

Stock Moving Averages

One Way To Know How Long To Hold, When To Fold

■ **A moving average smooths out the volatility that often characterizes daily stock or market price action.**

Cut your losses and let your profits run.

That oft-given advice may be easy to understand. But in a market driven by greed and fear, it's not so easy to follow.

There's always the temptation to take profits in a stock that may have its best move still ahead of it. Similarly, investors are frequently shaken out of top stocks when they pull back.

To ride a real winner—one that will double or triple or more—requires a lot of savvy.

One of the best technical tools to help investors stay on the winning side of trades, whether bullish or bearish, is a moving average line. Analysts use such averages to help determine whether a stock has moved up too quickly or is acting poorly and may head lower.

Investor's Business Daily includes 50-day moving average lines for the individual stock-price charts published each day atop the closing prices for the New York and American stock exchanges and the Nasdaq market.

A simple moving average is constructed by collecting the closing prices of a stock or market average over a fixed period of time and then calculating the arithmetic mean of those closing prices. The average is recalculated and plotted each day.

Smoothing Volatility

A moving average smooths out the volatility that often characterizes daily stock-price or stock-market actions. Generally speaking, a moving average using 25 trading sessions or fewer is considered short-term; from 26 to 100 would be intermediate-term; and 100 to 200 is long-term.

Investor's Business Daily uses 200-day moving averages throughout the newspaper. They are provided each day on the General Market Indicators page for the Dow Jones industrial average and the Standard & Poor's 500 and *Investor's Business Daily* 6000 indexes.

The Amex Market Value index and the Nasdaq composite index, which appear in their respective sections, also have 200-day lines. So does the *Investor's Business Daily* Fund Index in the mutual fund section. It also has 50-day moving average.

Finally, the five-year and one-year charts of stocks that appear daily on the "Industries In The News" page have both 200- and 50-day moving average lines.

The addition of the intermediate-term 50-day trend indicator for individual stocks was added at the request of readers.

Calculating Averages

The moving average used in the individual stock charts is simple. Each point on the moving average is calculated by using the average of the sum of the previous 50 closing prices.

There are other ways to calculate moving averages, such as weighted or exponential averages that may give more emphasis to the most recent price action.

A 50-day moving average is a good intermediate-term trend indicator. The first thing you should observe is its trend—up, down or sideways.

On the accompanying chart for Cerner Corp., the 50-day moving average line is the smooth thin line between the weekly (high-low-close) price line and the jagged Relative Strength line.

You can see how the stock has ridden above the 50-day average, only rarely cutting below it. This, obviously, is a powerful uptrend—one with a nearly straight-line trajectory not seen very often (which is not to say they aren't worth looking for).

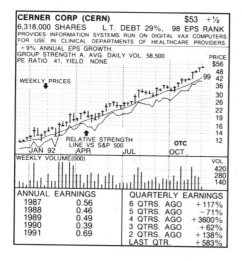

CERNER CORP (CERN) $53 +½
6,318,000 SHARES   L.T. DEBT 29%, 98 EPS RANK
PROVIDES INFORMATION SYSTEMS RUN ON DIGITAL VAX COMPUTERS
FOR USE IN CLINICAL DEPARTMENTS OF HEALTHCARE PROVIDERS.
+9% ANNUAL EPS GROWTH.
GROUP STRENGTH A, AVG. DAILY VOL. 58,500
PE RATIO 41, YIELD NONE

ANNUAL EARNINGS		QUARTERLY EARNINGS	
1987	0.56	6 QTRS. AGO	+117%
1988	0.46	5 QTRS. AGO	−71%
1989	0.49	4 QTRS. AGO	+3600%
1990	0.39	3 QTRS. AGO	+62%
1991	0.69	2 QTRS. AGO	+138%
		LAST QTR.	+583%

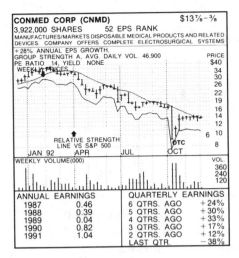

ANNUAL EARNINGS		QUARTERLY EARNINGS	
1987	0.46	6 QTRS. AGO	+24%
1988	0.39	5 QTRS. AGO	+30%
1989	0.04	4 QTRS. AGO	+33%
1990	0.82	3 QTRS. AGO	+17%
1991	1.04	2 QTRS. AGO	+12%
		LAST QTR.	−38%

The 50-day line, in fact, appears to have served as a floor off which the stock has bounced whenever it has weakened. An investor who owns the stock could feel comfortable holding it as long as it remained above the 50-day line that has proved so supportive.

If the stock broke down below that line, however, it may be an early sign that its long uptrend is not longer intact.

The Conmed Corp. chart is a case in point. After a huge run-up in 1991—during which its 50-day line served as a floor underneath the stock—Conmed breached the line in February 1992. From that point on, the 50-day became a ceiling through which the stock was unable to break.

Some people buy when the price of a stock crosses above the moving average line and sell or go short when it cuts below the line on increased volume.

You have to be careful, however. The Cerner and Conmed examples are used here because they are easy to follow. Most stocks haven't established such clear up- or down-trends. And when a stock moves sideways, it can cross its moving average line several times, causing traders to be whipsawed.

'Stocks In The News' Charts

Acknowledging How The Strong Get Stronger

■ **What seems high, or "expensive," to the majority often goes higher.**

Flanking the wide spectrum of stock-market investors are "bargain hunters" and "momentum players." Bargain hunters look for what, according to their analysis, appear to be "undervalued" issues. Momentum players, on the other hand, prowl for stocks that are rising rapidly.

Both methods can make money for their followers. But many top-performing money managers favor "leading" stocks in top-performing industry groups. At the same time, they avoid the underperformers, or "laggards."

These successful investors subscribe to the market adage that "the strong get stronger." Many are also aware of studies showing that stocks making "new highs"—that is, those reaching price levels not seen in a year or more—tend to continue their winning ways.

Reasons For New High

There are both fundamental and technical reasons for the success of stocks on the new-high list.

On a "fundamental" basis, a company whose stock is hitting new highs usually has something positive going for it. It might be a new product—a popular new software program, for example—that is enjoying strong acceptance.

Or there might be a significant change affecting its industry as a whole, such as the effect of trade measures on semiconductor sales. Management may be turning things around or a restructuring is starting to pay off in dramatically improved operating results.

The "technical" reason why stocks making new highs tend to do even better involves a basic principle of price structural analysis known as "overhead supply." This refers to stock that traded at higher levels in past months or years.

Assuming that other factors are positive, a stock that is already through its overhead supply is safer—that is, less likely to encounter selling pressure—than a stock approaching overhead supply.

Take a stock that falls from $50 a share to $20 over a period of time. When that stock bottoms and begins to turn up, investors who purchased it in the past higher-price area—say, in the $40 to $50 range tend to sell if the price rallies back and gives them an opportunity to recover losses.

Slow Selling

Investors also tend to be slow sellers. Some who wanted to sell but did not when the stock broke down, may sell as the stock rallies back. Furthermore, enough experienced professionals understand the principle to reinforce it by either selling or avoiding a stock as it approaches an overhead supply zone.

The increased supply and decreased demand make it harder for the stock to advance with as much momentum as it should.

A stock that has moved to new highs has no overhead supply. No one has bought it at higher price levels and the number of potential sellers has been reduced accordingly. The stock has, in the language of the market, "broken into the clear."

No one can predict how far it will eventually go once in new-high territory (though quantitative analysis could be done to try to determine a possible ceiling). But these "market leaders" sometimes will surprise investors by moving substantially higher than anyone thought.

One of the market's great paradoxes, studies have shown, is that what seems too high, or "expensive," to the majority often goes higher, and what seems low, or "cheap," often goes lower.

Investor's Business Daily was aware of the significance of

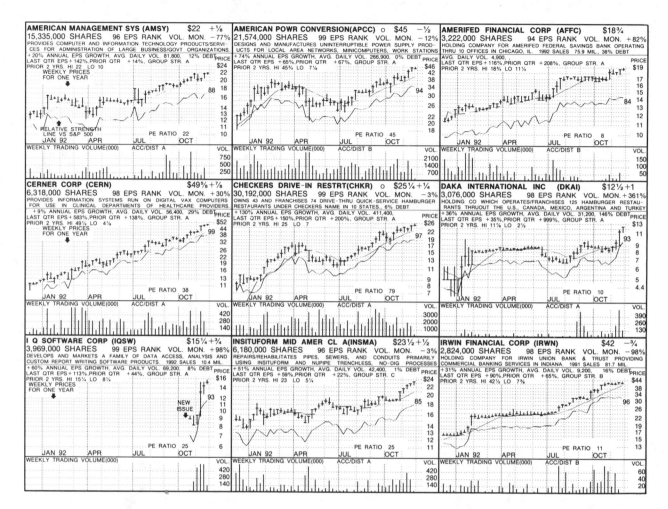

stocks making new highs. Thus, while other newspapers publish only a list of new highs every day, *Investor's Business Daily* gives its readers a far closer look at stocks that, despite their seemingly lofty prices, have considerably more upside potential.

Through the use of its sophisticated database of financial information and unique computer-graphics technology, *Investor's Business Daily* publishes charts of technical and fun-

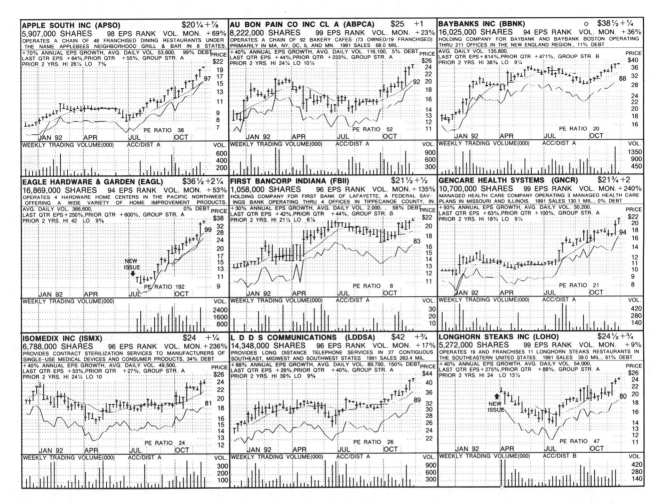

damental information about stocks on the new-high lists.
Though they occupy a small space, these charts contain a
wealth of information.

On the New York Stock Exchange, *Investor's Business Daily*
displays 30 stocks making new highs that are over $15 and have
moved up 1/2 point or more that day. If the number of stocks
making new highs is fewer than 30, the rest of the graphs shown
consist of those with the greatest percent increase in average

daily trading volume.

An additional 30 new-high charts on the American Stock Exchange and 30 on the OTC market are also displayed. The cutoff for the stocks are those over $12 and, on the Amex, those with a price change of 1/4 of a point for the day, and, on the OTC market, 3/8 of a point.

Again, if the number of new highs is less than 30 on the Amex or OTC, then stocks with the greatest percentage increase in volume are used. The stocks used in the charts have minimum prices in order to weed out cheap issues, which can be extremely risky, volatile and thinly traded.

When there are more than 30 stocks on the NYSE, Amex and OTC making new highs, those displayed are selected in order of Earnings Per Share rank—in effect, giving the reader a close-up look at the most profitable of the many companies making strong moves.

Overall Market Health

When the market itself is very strong, far more than 30 issues in each market are making new highs. In such an environment, it takes a very high EPS ranking for a stock to "qualify" for one of the 30 charts.

The average EPS rank of the 30 stocks shown, therefore, can be used to assess the overall health of the market. When the market is roaring, the most profitable companies are usually setting the pace, and it takes an EPS rank in the high 90s to qualify for a chart.

As the bull starts to tire, its original leaders come under profit-taking and fall off the new-high list. At that point, you will notice less-profitable companies coming to the fore and the average EPS rank of the 30 stocks start to drop.

You know a bull market is getting long in the tooth when stocks of laggard and less-profitable companies come on. You'll know that's happening when you start to see mediocre EPS ranks in the 60s or lower popping up on the 30 charts.

The excerpt is from a November 1992 issue of *Investor's*

Business Daily, when the Nasdaq market was climbing toward record highs. Note the high EPS ranks of the 18 stocks shown. The lowest was a lofty 94 and one in three had achieved the highest EPS rank possible—99.

"Stocks in the News" charts are also helpful in pinpointing leading industry groups. Note how many in the example are restaurants—Apple South, Au Bon Pain, Checkers Drive Ins, Daka International and Longhorn Steaks.

At the time, restaurants ranked 20th in year-to-date performance among the 197 industries tracked by *Investor's Business Daily* and sixth in six-month price performance.

There are few better places to go than "Stocks in the News" when the market, after a lengthy correction, turns and rallies. Many of the emerging leaders in the new bull market will show up quickly in these charts.

Of the 30 Nasdaq stocks that appeared on the charts in January 1991, at the outset of the explosive rally that coincided with the breakout of war in the Persian Gulf, 25 finished the year higher. Of those, the average gain was 143% (vs. 57% for the Nasdaq and 26% for the S&P 500).

Investors' Weekend Review

Sifting Out Leaders In Leading Groups

■ **Investors' Weekend Review presents a quick overview of leading stocks and industry groups in the market.**

As any stock investor knows, it's easy to be buried by the volume of information that spills out each day from financial markets. To many, especially those who aren't full-time tape watchers, the best time to analyze the market is over the weekend. To help them, *Investor's Business Daily* publishes each Friday a feature called "Investors' Weekend Review."

Presented in tabular form, it is a streamlined look at the stock market. It helps an investor get a quick overview of the market by identifying top-performing industry groups and the leading stocks in each, as well as key institutional owners of those stocks.

Leading Groups

Investor's Business Daily divides the market into 197 industry groups, which are then ranked based on the price performances of their component stocks. Groups are assigned Relative Strength rankings based on their performances over the previous 12 months.

Group ranking is critical. Studies show many of the top-performing stocks come from market-leading industries. That would mean they had a group Relative Strength of 75 or better.

After identifying top-performing groups, "Investors' Weekend Review" lists all stocks within those groups selling for more than $7 and with a Relative Strength and Earnings Per Share rank above 80. "Investor's Weekend Review" further pares the list by excluding those trading at more than 15% below their 12-

month highs.

The $7 cutoff eliminates cheap stocks. The 80 Relative Strength and EPS rankings narrow the screen to top performers based on price action and profit growth.

By additionally showing only the issues within 15% of their 12-month price highs, "Investors' Weekend Review" highlights those in position to break into new high ground.

That's a positive because it means there's no overhead supply (people who have bought at a higher price who will want to sell in order to break even). Stocks making new highs have the capability to race ahead strongly and become tremendous winners.

"Investors' Weekend Review" also lists the exchanges where those stocks are traded.

Price-to-earnings ratios are given to provide an idea of how the marketplace is valuing various companies and their rivals in a given industry.

"Investors' Weekend Review" also shows each stock's weekly price change through Thursday, the Thursday close and the percentage increase in daily volume compared with the average over the previous 50 days.

Institutional Sponsorship

One of the most intriguing features of "Investors' Weekend Review" is the listing of the best-performing mutual fund with the largest position in each stock.

The fact that a stock has institutional sponsorship is important because it takes strong demand to push a stock's price higher. And institutions such as mutual funds, pension funds, insurance companies, banks and private investment firms can provide that demand.

Many investors view the lack of sponsorship as a real negative, because it may mean investment firms have looked at the company and its stock and have rejected it for one reason or another.

The quality of sponsorship is especially important.

Institutional ownership by top-performing mutual funds provide further assurance that a company and its stock have something good going for them.

Stochastic Oscillators

Not As Esoteric As They Sound

■ **The stochastic oscillator gives excellent buy and sell signals when a market is moving in a choppy, sideways fashion.**

The word "stochastic" sounds hypermodern and, to the average investor, a little intimidating. But its meaning is simple, and if used properly it can help with market trading.

The word describes a price momentum indicator that was developed in the late 1970s to help traders pinpoint tops and bottoms more accurately.

It was first used in this context by George Lane, president of Investment Educators of Des Plaines, Ill., and it comes from the Greek *stochastikos*—meaning "skillful in aiming."

To help readers, *Investor's Business Daily* in 1991 broke new ground for newspapers by adding to its daily futures charts the 14-day stochastic oscillator.

"When I saw those price momentum charts in the paper, I nearly stood up in the train and applauded," recalls Ken Spence, market analyst at Salomon Brothers Inc. in New York. "It was wonderful to see them."

Spence studies stochastic momentum charts extensively in his technical work.

"I think it's a big step forward for the average newspaper reader," he says. "Price momentum charts give valuable information to a reader without them spending a lot of money on an expensive computer system."

The stochastic oscillator measures—on a percentage basis—where a futures contract's or a security's price is in relation to the total price range for a selected number of days.

The stochastic data are plotted on a chart with 100 at the top and 0 at the bottom. Two stochastic lines are shown—the %F, the raw data, and the %S, a moving average. The F stands for fast, the S for slow. In *Investor's Business Daily*, the chart is displayed directly below the futures contract price chart.

When the stochastic line is rising, that means the price momentum of the contract or security is increasing. Conversely, when the line is declining, it indicates price momentum is down.

Like any tool, the price momentum oscillator can be misused. In the hands of a wise analyst, it can be helpful in timing entry into a position.

Using The Oscillator

One simple way to use the oscillator is to buy when the %S value drops below 20 and then turns up and moves above 20. On the other side, a sell signal (or a short play) would be flashed if the %S rose above 80 and then fell below 80.

The stochastic oscillator gives excellent buy and sell signals when a market is moving in a choppy, sideways fashion.

Investor's Business Daily uses a 14-day stochastic, meaning the calculations cover 14-day periods. Some sophisticated technical analysts will adjust the oscillator to fit the historic cyclical moves of the security or contract in question.

For example, if a security makes a price peak about every 20 days, the stochastic oscillator could be changed from 14 days to 10 days, so it could more accurately peg tops and bottoms. If the cycle peaks are 60 days apart, then a 30-day oscillator would work best.

A second way to use the stochastic oscillator is to wait for a setup when both the %S and %F fall below 20. When the %F line crosses the %S line, it is a buy signal.

The reverse works on selling. Wait for both the %S and %F to climb over 80 and then, when the %F cuts below the %S, sell.

This method can catch the tops and bottoms very well, especially in fast- moving markets. But the drawback is that stochastics can give many false signals.

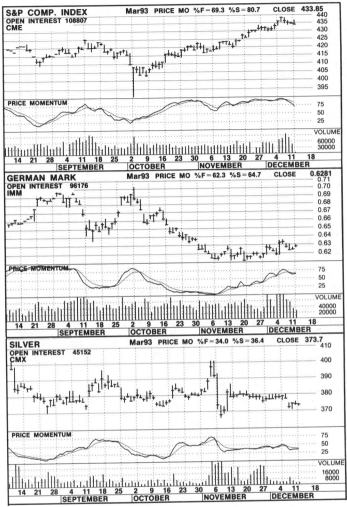

The third way to use the stochastic is to look for divergences in the trend of the oscillator and the price of the security.

If the stochastic oscillator is below 25 and then turns up and makes a higher short-term high—even though the security's price has not—a buy signal is flashed.

A sell signal is given when the oscillator is above 75 and makes a lower short-term low, even though the security hasn't.

Analyst Spence cautions that the stochastic should not be used alone in the trading of securities.

"You should study volume, open interest, and be aware of the trend of the security," he says. "You want to see as many indicators as possible working with your position, even the fundamentals."

But "if the stochastic goes over 80," Spence adds, "it's usually a good signal not to chase a security as a buy. Likewise, if the oscillator drops below 20, you don't want to go short. It's too late."

Spence likes to use a nine-unit stochastic oscillator, and he sets it to follow some markets on hourly, daily, weekly and monthly bases. He does that to get a feel for the market's momentum for short, intermediate and long terms.

Many futures traders use intraday data—five-minute or 15-minute charts. *Investors Business Daily* provides daily data.

Trending Markets

The stochastic oscillator is not the ultimate indicator. It does have its Achilles' heel. That is, it has to be interpreted entirely differently in a trending market, or one that has an explosive move up or down.

Marc Chaikin, an analyst at Instinet in New York, estimates that most markets are in a trending phase—either upward or downward—33% of the time and go sideways 66%. High-momentum phases happen about 15% of the time.

The stock market's explosive run-up in January and February of 1991 was an example of an "explosive phase." Using the basic 20-80 stochastic buy-sell rule would not have worked well. It may have taken investors out of the long side too soon.

"One would have to take into account a rocketlike move in a security or a market and use perhaps a stochastic break under 50 as a sell signal," added Spence. "An initial, powerful up move often signals a continuation of the trend higher. The same idea goes for a sharp break to the downside."

In gently trending markets, the stochastic 80-20 rule can be used to find entry points. The important thing to remember is to go with the general trend. Never try to "scalp" a position using the stochastic buy and sell signals by going against the trend.

"I think the stochastic oscillator is a good contribution to market analysis, but it has to be used properly," says Spence. "It can help you evaluate the internal strength of a security."

Investment Strategy

Valuing Growth Stocks

One Analyst's Rigorous Method

■ **There are relatively precise measures for determining what a growth company is worth and its chances for a health future.**

Figuring out what small-capitalization growth stocks are worth typically calls for a bit of art along with economic science.

Hours of numbers-crunching can come to naught if a growth company unexpectedly announces that its latest product has the intrinsic value of snake oil, or if its head of research and development, who also happens to be chairman, chief executive and president, retires to go deep-sea fishing.

Still, there are relatively precise measures for determining what a growth company is worth and its chances for a healthy future.

10 Characteristics

For L. Keith Mullins, a growth-stock specialist for more than a decade, the process involves a rigorous set of criteria designed to evaluate specific growth stocks and the entire market in which they operate.

Formerly with Morgan Stanley & Co. and now with Smith Barney, Harris Upham & Co., Mullins begins the process by employing 10 characteristics to identify a promising emerging company:

■ Expected revenue and earnings expansion of 20% or more in each of the next five years. The growth should come from existing operations, not acquisitions.

■ Market capitalization of less than $1 billion.

- Total debt below 40% of its market capitalization (the price of its stock multiplied by the number of common shares outstanding).
- Above-average profitability with an annual return on equity approximating 20%. This reduces the need to raise money by issuing more stock and diluting the positions of existing shareholders.
- The No. 1 or No. 2 spot in a market niche, which reduces vulnerability to price competition.
- Barriers to entry by competitors, including established distribution channels, proprietary databases, large research costs, management expertise and exceptional customer service. Patents, however, are poor barriers.
- A strong management team that does not rely on a single entrepreneur.
- Conservative accounting with a minimum of deferred expenses.
- Several products, which lessen the reliance on one blockbuster item.
- Recurring revenues from such sources as licensing agreements, royalties, high customer renewals and maintenance contracts. (Not as important as the preceding factors.)

Once a company fits Mullins' profile, the analyst then uses three techniques to determine a stock's value: absolute value, relative value and business environment.

Absolute Value

Establishing absolute value begins with discounting a company's future earnings in light of long-term interest rates.

Mullins then applies a multiple to that earnings stream based on the company's financial condition, growth rate and future prospects.

He emphasizes that quality growth stocks will typically carry high price-to-earnings ratios.

"Our experience," Mullins says, "suggests that those investment opportunities that appear 'cheap' often are overwhelmingly cheap for legitimate reasons.

"You have to pay up for quality," he explains. "Even the stocks that seem to be overvalued on a short-term basis ... those are the ones I can hold for an extended period."

He cited Cisco Systems Inc. as an example. The supplier of computer networking products at one point was trading at about 30 times its trailing 12-month earnings—a multiple many analysts and investors consider too high. But that was about the time Cisco embarked on a 160% advance.

The stock wouldn't have looked as pricey, Mullins noted, had the multiple been calculated using expected earnings for the coming 12 months. That's why Mullins always uses this formula when determining P-E ratios.

"On growth stocks," he points out, "you are paying for the future."

The last calculation for determining absolute value is the P-E ratio to projected growth rate. For example, if a company has an expected annual earnings growth rate of 25% and a P-E of 15, its P-E to projected growth rate is 60%, or 15 divided by 0.25.

In general, a stock is attractively priced when its P-E to projected growth rate is below 75% and overpriced at 125% or more.

Relative Value

Mullins uses two criteria to establish the relative value of growth stocks, which provide a clue to how a stock might perform compared with all other issues.

The analyst starts by comparing the P-E of the T. Rowe Price New Horizons Fund, which represents a diversified basket of growth stocks, to the P-E of the Standard & Poor's 500-stock index.

The fund has traded at between one and two times the S&P index since 1960, reaching its peak in 1983.

Growth stocks then went into a period of prolonged decline and finally came back into favor last October. However, the fund indicator is still trading at only 1.14 times the S&P index, which means it has plenty of upside potential, Mullins says.

After comparing those two P-Es, Mullins then determines how, on average, investors are valuing earnings growth for growth stocks compared with the S&P 500.

(Some other experts, it should be noted, no longer think the New Horizons fund is a useful proxy for small-cap growth issues.)

Market Variables

Finally, Mullins looks at external market variables.

A high level of initial public offerings is viewed as a bad omen because it diverts buying power from existing growth stocks. The danger point is reached when IPOs make up 50% of the new equities market.

The analyst also monitors aggressive growth mutual funds to determine the sentiments of fund managers and their customers. New money committed to these funds should be neither markedly high nor markedly low at any one time.

Although many mutual funds are already fully invested, Mullin says they are receiving a steady flow of new client money, and that helps maintain demand for smaller stocks.

Also, pension funds are starting to show greater interest in growth stocks.

Mullins is always on the lookout, however, for a large number of short positions on Nasdaq stocks. The more shorts there are, the greater the likelihood of negative rumors that can quickly crush a small-capitalization issue.

But Mullins' research helps give him the confidence to hold onto stocks through the sharp, and often short-term, corrections that plague growth issues. That's important, he says, because successful growth stocks are most rewarding when held for at least two years.

"It's very difficult to buy and sell these stocks, so you have to be able to hold them," he says. "You ride your winners until they're old nags."

Industry Prices

Isolating The Best-Performing Groups

■ **Stocks in the top 100 groups will rise more in price than the lower 100. Stocks in the top 50 will move up substantially more.**

When searching for a stock that will be a top performer, it often happens that an industry group will contain not just one outstanding candidate, but several.

This market development is what is known on Wall Street as pinpointing a "leading" industry group.

The tendency to find strong stocks grouped together has been noted by market analysts for years. The development is quite natural and usually due to something positive, either fundamentally or technically, taking place within an industry.

The powerful influence of group behavior is among the reasons *Investor's Business Daily* makes it a point to closely monitor the performance of no fewer than 197 industries.

Over the course of a week, the groups are listed in alphabetical order and ranked by six-month and year-to-date performance.

Indexes compiled for each group, and the index change from the prior session, are shown each day. So is the number of stocks in each group, an earnings rank for the group vs. the other 196 groups, the group's relative price strength vs. all other groups, and its percentage sales growth.

Leading Groups

Below the rankings, *Investor's Business Daily* highlights a leading group by providing a chart showing its price and volume action for the past five months and a table showing all stocks in the group (space permitting) ranked by their Earnings Per

Share and Relative Strength ranks.

A brief story on developments in the industry and its leading companies is also included.

A statistical study done by *Investor's Business Daily* has shown that stocks in the top 100 groups will rise more in price, on balance, than the lower 100. In addition, stocks in the top 50 will move up substantially more in price than the lower 50.

Investor's Business Daily tracks 197 groups in all—far more than the 80 or so groups used, for example, by Standard & Poor's—because there are many new and important industries emerging.

Twenty percent of the best-performing stocks in the 1991 bull market, for example, were in businesses that either didn't exist or weren't large enough ten years earlier to be considered a separate industry for stock-grouping purposes.

Segmented Industries

Investor's Business Daily's more-specific groupings enable readers to see how segments within wide-ranging industries are faring.

"High-technology" stocks in general, for example, were leaders in the fall rally of 1992. But *Investor's Business Daily* readers who kept an eye on the group rankings knew that the strongest of the strongest were those in the relatively new field of computer networking.

They were followed by makers of computer peripheral equipment and software and by providers of computer services. Mainframe manufacturers, by contrast, languished near the bottom of the list.

In all, *Investor's Business Daily* tracks eight computer groups, not including semiconductors and other electronics segments.

One of the most striking examples of group leadership was in 1991, when seven of the top ten industries were in the medical field. Eight were in the top 12, and all the 11 medical groups tracked by the newspaper finished in the top 25%.

Earnings Season

A Good Time To Be Alert

■ **If a stock is acting exceptionally well, there's a good possibility a positive earnings surprise could be coming up.**

One of the most important short-term influences on a stock is the quarterly earnings report.

Wall Street often rewards companies showing strong earnings gains or positive surprises by sending their prices higher and punishes those that disappoint by sending their shares south.

Knowing when results are due can help investors tremendously. And to help you zero in on forthcoming quarterly earnings, *Investor's Business Daily* has built in special features to its already superior stock tables.

If a company's earnings are due in the next four weeks, the letter "k" appears at the end of its stock listing. The "k" lets you know it's time to be alert.

Watching The Calendar

If a stock you're holding will report earnings soon, it's wise to be aware of the actual date they may come in. Also, you should try to find out what analysts are forecasting and what might constitute a positive or negative surprise.

Since the "k" shows up about a month before the actual earnings report, it's a good idea to keep close tabs on how the stock is performing. If it's acting exceptionally well—up sharply on heavy volume—over several days there's a good possibility a positive earnings surprise could be coming up.

If the stock is unusually weak, perhaps down a few points in heavy trading, it could mean trouble ahead in the form of disappointing results. If the stock shows no significant change and no unusual volume, then you'd assume that nothing special is in the offing.

Many public companies hint of their progress to industry analysts. That means word of how a company is doing can affect its share price before earnings are released. As a result, the result may have already been taken into account by traders.

An experienced and wise investor knows this and looks for it, whether it portends good or bad results.

Also, if a company's earnings report appears to be very late, it could be a sign that bad news is on the way. Companies have a tendency to delay reporting disappointing earnings or big losses.

Hyphens

When the company finally reports earnings, and those results appear in that day's *Investor's Business Daily*, a hyphen (-) appears at the end of the stock listing.

The "k" notation can also flag investors to new investment opportunities. If a stock is beginning to act badly prior to an earnings report, it could be a candidate for a short sale. But further research should be done and the general condition of the market should be taken into consideration.

If the stock is behaving strongly prior to an earnings release, it could be a buy. But again, that's only after further investigation. If you're taking this approach, it's a good idea to scan *Investor's Business Daily's* stock tables each day for those issues with a "k" that are acting poorly or strongly on heavy volume.

Not every stock that acts well prior to an earnings report will show better results. There are always the genuine surprises. But generally the activity of a stock ahead of earnings should be watched carefully.

Earnings Reports

Separating The 'Ups' From The 'Downs'

■ By scanning the earnings list for companies that have shown a rise in earnings, you can often spot an emerging growth firm.

In analyzing stock-price trends, one of the most closely watched fundamentals is earnings growth.

The concept is simple: A company whose profit is growing will accumulate more assets and become more valuable, and its stock should rise. Conversely, a company that's losing money will see its assets shrink and will become less valuable, and its stock price should decline.

That's theory. But there are other factors that come into play.

Earnings growth alone can not be taken as an indication that a stock will rise. The stock's current price, for example, must be taken into consideration. It may be too high already after being bid up by other investors. That's why analysts calculate share price-to-earnings ratios and compare P-E's among companies in the same industry.

Still, there's no denying the fact that a company with improving earnings stands a good chance of seeing its stock price bid up. A study of the greatest stocks of the last 40 years by William O'Neil & Co., a sister company to Investor's Business Daily Inc., found the most important common denominator to be substantial profit growth.

Publishing Results

Major business newspapers have long recognized the importance of publishing corporate financial results. Many of the top stories are often about dramatic changes in profitability. Also, many carry tables listing reported earnings.

Investor's Business Daily realized the importance of earnings reports, too. Earnings developments that are especially important will often be noted in the "News Digest" on the front page, and inside stories elaborate on the results of various companies.

Investor's Business Daily also includes earnings reports—but in a way not done by other newspapers. The results are divided into two groups—ups and downs—and are then listed alphabetically.

In addition, *Investor's Business Daily* calculates and boldfaces the percentage change in quarterly earnings per share—another service provided no where else.

Finally, lists of companies showing the biggest profit gains ("Best Ups") and the worst results ("Most Downs") are broken out for quick reference.

Ups And Downs

Why the separation of ups from downs? So the reader can readily see which companies are producing positive results and which aren't. Most often, those with improving results are the better-performing stocks. And market laggards are often those firms whose financial results are deteriorating.

Investor's Business Daily's earnings report table is a good place to find new investment ideas. By scanning the list for companies that have shown a rise in earnings, especially a big rise, you can spot a new emerging growth firm and a potentially good investment. Of course, further analysis of the stock and the company's other fundamentals is needed.

To help the reader further identify those companies with the best results, *Investor's Business Daily* puts a star beside quarterly earnings gains of 20% or more.

Studies have shown that, in general, companies reporting at least a 20% growth in earnings are among the fastest-growing firms and their stocks among the best performers.

When a firm reports "good" earnings, it's important to check the data to see if there are any extraordinary items that may have affected the comparison.

A company may report a giant increase in earnings. But the fine print may show that most of it came from a one-time, non-recurring event, such as the sale of real estate. What the investor is interested in is the ongoing profitability of corporate operations.

Earnings Record

Also, it's wise to research the earnings record of the firm, taking particular notice of what its rate of growth has been in previous quarters.

At first glance, a company reporting earnings up 20% seems to be doing well. But if its historical growth rate is 60%, the latest results could be signaling a significant slowdown or decelerating in profitability. Strong stocks often top out at such junctures.

It's also helpful to know if the year-earlier results—those against which the latest numbers are being compared—were strong or weak.

A company may report an impressive increase in the latest quarter. But the comparison may have been unusually "easy" because the year-earlier results were unusually depressed. Similarly, a solid earnings gain in the latest quarter may be even more impressive if the year-earlier quarter was also a strong one.

Always make sure the most recent quarter's results are being compared. Some companies, trying to put their best foot forward, report six-month or full-year results and leave it to the reader to figure out what the latest quarter did. The six-month or full-year results may be up, but the latest quarter may have been down.

Wall Street Expectations

It's also helpful to know what earnings "the Street"—or securities analysts—were expecting. Sometimes a stock will fall because the "good" earnings were not good enough.

You should also check the stock's price action for the day to see how the market reacted to the earnings news. Going a step further, check the price action during the previous days to see if there was a rise in anticipation of the results.

Sometimes a stock will move up ahead of the news and then sell off on the actual report. But at other times it won't, and the stock will be propelled 20% or 25% higher if the results are much better than expected.

Earnings are reported at the end of every quarter. The months of April, July, October and January are the heaviest period for earnings reports. Some firms, most notably the retailers, have fiscal years ending Jan. 31, so their profits are released in May, August, November and February.

Largest % Increase In Volume

A Giant Leap Forward In 'Most-Active' Lists

■ **Unusual volume generally reveals accumulation or distribution by institutions that buy stocks in large quantities.**

For decades, a fixture in most newspapers that carry stock tables has been the "most active" list, a rundown of issues that traded the most shares in any given day.

And for decades, the list has been made up of the same companies—such as IBM, General Motors, General Electric and AT&T. They are, indeed, widely held and of interest to many people, including their millions of shareholders.

But they are actively traded mainly for one reason: They are huge companies with hundreds of millions of shares outstanding.

Only rarely, however, do the conventional most-active lists reveal information of value to investors. They do not, for example, show trading in the innovative small- and medium-size companies that are fast-assuming market leadership.

Investor's Business Daily publishes a list of most-active stocks, but that's about where the similarity ends.

Greatest % Increase

It goes a step further by screening and displaying those issues that show the greatest percentage increase in volume above their average daily trading level.

Shown in special tables are the 60 NYSE stocks, the 100 Nasdaq stocks and the 15 Amex issues "With The Greatest % Rise In Volume."

Stocks that are up in price on big volume are displayed at the top of each list, and those down on big volume are at the bottom of each list.

(So that the tables aren't dominated by cheaper, lower-grade issues, only those over $15 a share on the NYSE and over $12 a share on the Nasdaq and Amex are shown.)

Investment Ideas

These tables can be a major source of investment ideas. Unusual volume generally reveals accumulation or distribution by institutions that buy stocks in large quantities.

Heavy trading—such as that which generally puts a stock on the percent volume leaders—often precedes major price moves. An additional screen boldfaces those stocks on the list that are moving up and also rank 80 or higher in both Earnings Per Share and Relative Strength rank.

The big-volume gainers can also show accumulation or distribution in industry groups. The example was taken from a November 1992 edition.

Savvy investors will notice that no fewer than a half-dozen stocks on the list were life insurers—American Heritage, Leucadia, John Alden, Life Re, Broad and Lincoln.

60 NYSE Stocks With Greatest % Rise In Volume

Compared to stock's last 50 days avg. daily trading volume. Stocks over $15 and ½ pt. change. Stocks up in price listed first. Stocks up with EPS & Relative Strength 80 or more are **boldfaced**.

EPS Rnk	Rel. Str.	Last 52-Week High	Last 52-Week Low	Stock Name	Stock Symbol	Closing Price	Price Change	Group Str.	PE Ratio	Volume (100s)	% Change In Vol.
79	61	32½	22	Amer Heritage Life	AHL	29¾	+ ½	B	14	54,9	+6000
50	29	28½	18	A L Labs Inc Cl A	BMD	20⅞	+ 2⅛	C	55	970,4	+841
95	70	22¼	19½	CMAC Investment	CMT	24	+ 1⅞	B	9	352,0	+821
59	93	27⅛	12⅝	Caldor Corp	CLD	27⅞	+ ¾	A	10	440,0	+710
77	38	38¼	24⅜	Vivra Inc	V	28⅛	+ 1⅛	B	20	259,2	+610
68	47	24	18⅜	Intl Aluminum Corp	IAL	21¼	+ ½	C	59	5,8	+544
84	63	59⅝	35	Rohm & Haas Co o	ROH	55¼	+ 1½	E	17	466,5	+379
84	58	45⅞	34¼	Carlisle Cos Inc	CSL	43½	+ ⅝	C	14	21,5	+348
44	33	32⅜	24¼	Chemed Corp	CHE	26½	+ ½	C	17	128,2	+336
99	**91**	**70½**	**34⅞**	**Leucadia Natnl Corp**	**LUK**	**70⅝**	**+ ¾**	**B**	**6**	**50,0**	**+273**
83	69	34	22½	Bard C R Inc o	BCR	33½	+ 2½	B	26	528,3	+265
	43	16⅜	14⅝	Muniyield Florida Fd	MYF	15⅜	+ ½	D	..	15,1	+260
99	**81**	**18⅝**	**13¾**	**John Alden Finl Corp**	**JA**	**19**	**+ ⅝**	**B**	**4**	**262,0**	**+259**
96	56	26⅞	24¼	Life Re Corp	LRE	27	+ ⅝	B	13	128,2	+225
95	**98**	**29¾**	**8⅜**	**E M C Corp Mass o**	**EMC**	**30⅛**	**+ ⅞**	**B**	**35**	**712,6**	**+222**
12	96	35½	8⅜	Alexanders Inc	ALX	37¼	+ 2⅜	A	..	92,4	+220
22	12	33	19	English China Clays	ENC	21¾	+ 1⅛	D	13	8,5	+204
84	74	37	15⅝	Russ Berrie & Co	RUS	28⅜	+ ⅝	B	7	165,0	+189
70	81	43	26½	Barnett Banks Inc o	BBI	43½	+ ⅝	A	18	591,3	+188
14	23	30½	20⅛	Barclays Plc ADR	BCS	23	+ ⅝	E	20	17,6	+163
70	76	19	12	Lubys Cafeterias	LUB	19⅞	+ ⅞	A	17	139,1	+159
51	50	37½	29	Ameron Inc Del	AMN	35	+ ½	C	18	21,2	+159
96	**89**	**24¾**	**13⅞**	**Broad Inc o**	**BRO**	**25½**	**+ ¾**	**A**	**14**	**208,7**	**+137**
95	**84**	**30¼**	**17⅜**	**Centex Corp o**	**CTX**	**30**	**+ 1**	**C**	**20**	**310,4**	**+135**
95	**82**	**46¾**	**31½**	**M G I C Invt Corp o**	**MTG**	**46⅜**	**+ ⅞**	**B**	**14**	**153,3**	**+124**
43	52	42⅝	35⅛	Heinz H J Co o	HNZ	40¼	+ ¾	B	20	800,3	+116
74	29	63¾	52⅞	Mapco Inc o	MDA	54⅛	+ 1⅛	B	13	121,4	+114
47	69	41⅛	30⅛	Block H & R Inc o	HRB	39¼	+ 1⅛	A	27	492,6	+113
71	77	70¼	49⅜	Lincoln Natnl Corp o	LNC	69⅞	+ ¾	A	11	153,8	+112
79	73	70½	53½	Tambrands Inc o	TMB	69½	+ ⅝	B	24	203,4	+111
90	**84**	**42¼**	**22½**	**Marshall Industries**	**MI**	**40⅝**	**+ ⅝**	**A**	**16**	**36,9**	**+110**
56	29	59⅜	28⅛	Gap Inc o	GPS	34½	+ ¾	A	22	1,627,5	+103
98	**85**	**15½**	**10**	**Mercury Finance Co**	**MFN**	**15⅞**	**+ ½**	**A**	**32**	**109,2**	**+102**
31	52	41	33⅞	Laclede Gas Co	LG	39⅜	+ ¾	B	16	10,0	+100
8	10	43½	15¼	Chiquita Brands Intl o	CQB	16¼	+ ½	B	..	332,8	+99
65	63	54¾	38¼	Briggs&Stratton Cp o	BGG	49⅞	+ ⅞	C	14	67,9	+99
81	21	30¾	18	Spaghetti Wrehouse	SWH	20⅜	+ 1	A	22	125,0	+99
48	21	33⅞	11¾	Jenny Craig Inc	JC	17¼	+ 1¼	A	11	88,8	+97
27	13	30	18⅞	Banco Bilbao Vizcay	BBV	20	+ ⅝	E	..	19,9	+91
37	32	27½	22⅝	Potomac Elec Power	POM	23⅝	+ ⅝	D	15	292,9	+85
77	63	40⅛	30¾	Dial Corp o	DL	39⅝	+ ⅝	C	15	128,9	+82
95	75	38¾	25⅛	Century Telephone o	CTL	39¾	+ 1⅛	D	25	133,5	+77

Price-Earnings Ratios

How Pros Determine The 'E' In P-E

■ **What constitutes fair value is subjective, and it varies by company, stock, market environment and interest rates.**

If there is one subject growth-stock managers agree on, it is that earnings are critical and evaluating them properly is just as important.

No matter how splashy its product or charismatic its leader, if a growth company can't produce strong earnings growth, professional money managers say its stock isn't worth owning.

"If you don't make the earnings, no one's going to dance with you," said Art Bonnel, portfolio manager of the MIM Stock Appreciation Fund in Reno, Nev.

Keeping track of earnings is a daily exercise for many professional investors. The latest estimates are constantly compared with the stock's price to determine price-earnings ratios.

"The key to investing is to get your hands around earnings," said Jeffrey Malet, president of Pacific Century Advisers in La Jolla, Calif. "It's a very simple question, but it cuts to the very basics of investing."

Fair Value

The P-E ratio is one barometer investors use to determine whether a stock is fairly valued, and it helps many decide whether to buy or sell a stock. But what constitutes fair value is subjective, and it varies with the type of company, the stock market environment and interest rates.

A loose rule of thumb is to hold a stock as long as its earnings growth rate meets or exceeds its P-E ratio, some argue. If a company's earnings growth rate is 35% a year, a P-E of 35 is justified.

Malet is willing to give stocks more room. He doesn't get nervous until the P-E exceeds the growth rate by 30%.

When it comes to biotechnology companies, Malet is even more lenient. He allows a much higher P-E ratio for these stocks because of the enormous earnings potential of the industry.

The P-E multiples of biotechs are high because many of the companies have minimal earnings. What's more, some companies are continuing research and are not expected to turn a profit for several years.

This type of investing can produce enormous rewards, but it also carries substantial risks. Many biotech companies will fold before they make a dime, Malet says.

Interest rates also help determine an acceptable P-E level. Lower interest rates are good for financial markets in general, but they are especially valuable for fast-growing companies because the value of their earnings going forward increases faster.

"In this kind of environment, where interest rates are low, I would expect growth companies to perform better," Malet says.

Earnings Predictions

With all the emphasis on profits, it's not surprising that research analysts spend so much of their time predicting earnings for the coming quarter or year.

Nevertheless, their estimates often vary by several pennies, if not much more. And, all too often, Wall Street estimates miss the mark altogether.

That's why many money managers try to either gather their own estimates or at least do a substantial amount of work to confirm the Wall Street consensus.

What many look for are companies that are likely to beat the consensus estimates, thus producing a sharp acceleration in their stock price. If a company merely meets the expectations, the reaction is usually a big yawn.

"It's extremely important not to take the Wall Street consensus estimate as a given," says Malet, "because in most cases the stock price fully incorporates that estimate."

So how do professional investors establish their earnings estimates?

Like others, David J. Evans, vice president of research for Robertson Stephens Investment Management Inc., starts by talking to the company.

"What you're looking for is management's ability to execute their plan," Evans said. "We visit a lot of companies, and we attend a lot of IPO roadshows."

Cup Of Coffee

The most revealing information about a firm often comes over a cup of coffee with company executives. Evans notes that during one meeting, a chief executive and a chief financial officer disagreed on their company's direction—a warning flag that trouble lay ahead.

"Part of it is an understanding of how people think and what they've done before," he says. "Who have they got on their board, and do they listen to people who could help them?"

Evans also looks at the track record of both the management and the investors who provided the start-up money for a firm.

Once he determines that a company has sound management and good products, Evans concentrates on revenues and earnings for the next four quarters. Like most other growth-stock managers, Evans is not concerned with trailing earnings.

A growth stock's ability to move higher will depend almost solely on its ability to produce earnings acceleration of at least 20% a quarter going forward, not on its past profits.

That's not to say that trailing earnings are irrelevant. Several quarters of accelerating profits help confirm that a company is on a steady growth path.

Talking with analysts and executives about a company's earnings is important, Malet says, but that's just the beginning.

Analysts may not have done their homework, or a firm may be hiding negative information in the hope that its fortunes will turn before the next earnings report. Or it simply may not have sufficiently sharp accounting controls to pick up deterioration in profits.

To double-check the estimates, Malet calls the company's vendors and its customers, or he sends employees into the field to see how well merchandise is selling.

"The bottom line is that it's always important to have a multitude of sources," he said, "because the earnings that most people use in their estimates are not always correct."

Again, his goal is to find companies whose earnings are going to exceed expectations, either in the coming quarter or beyond. The strategy has given Malet's Pacific Horizon Aggressive Growth Fund an A+ rating from *Investor's Business Daily* for three-year performance.

But it's not the only approach that works. Bonnel's MIM Stock Appreciation Fund, another A+ performer, uses a different tack.

Bonnell invests in companies right after they have announced earnings surprises. That way he's almost sure to get a winner.

"I want to be on the bandwagon as it's leaving," he said. "I don't want to be the first on it. I want to see the company earn money. If it's not, I move out of it immediately."

Forward-Looking P-Es

Helping Shrug Off The 'Overvalued' Stigma

■ **A company's future, not past, earnings are most relevant to picking growth stocks.**

Many stocks appear pricey based on trailing 12-month earnings, but top managers say that measure has little relevance for successful growth-stock investing.

"In a growth stock portfolio, looking at trailing earnings is kindergarten," said John M. Hartwell, manager of the Keystone America Hartwell Emerging Growth Fund. "You cannot value (growth stocks) based on past earnings."

But using companies' trailing 12-month earnings remains a fairly common method for analyzing stocks. And the practice often results in market observers incorrectly declaring certain top-performing stocks to be "overvalued."

Growth stock managers acknowledge that there are times when bargains in the market are harder find. But even then, they say, there are still plenty of attractive issues available.

Future Earnings

It is a company's future, not past, earnings that are most relevant to picking growth stocks, managers emphasize. They say trailing earnings are of limited use, except perhaps to the extent that they give an indication of the predictability of a company's performance.

Moreover, a company's price-earnings ratio should be analyzed using its future earnings, not its past, managers say.

Other factors that may affect what a manager is willing to pay for a stock include whether a company operates in a niche business, prevailing interest rates and a company's size.

"I'm obviously not investing on trailing earnings," Hartwell said. The stocks in his fund in early 1992 had an average P-E of 53 based on their earnings in the prior 12 months.

The portfolio's P-E likely was skewed by his positions in biotechnology and cellular stocks, where trailing earnings are meaningless because the companies have little or no profits, he notes.

The Hartwell Emerging Growth Fund was rated A+ by *Investor's Business Daily* for its 1989-91 performance.

As basic parameters, Hartwell looks for companies with annual earnings growth of at least 30% and stocks where the P-E ratio, based on the current year's estimated earnings, does not exceed the company's growth rate.

One of his top picks was software developer Cisco Systems Inc. Hartwell estimated the company would earn $2.60 a share in 1992. With the stock trading at the time at about 84, it had a P-E of 45 based on trailing 12-month earnings of $1.86 a share.

But its P-E dropped to 32 based on its estimated earnings for the following 12 months. The stock remained attractive, he says, because the company's earnings growth rate had been and would continue to be well above 50%.

"The multiple on past 12 months' earnings is only in the newspaper—not on any investment managers' sheets of paper," said Michael Arends, co-manager of the Chicago-based (and A+ rated) Kemper Growth Fund and three other portfolios.

Arends says the stocks in his growth portfolio had a 1992 estimated average earnings growth rate of 25% and an average 1992 estimated P-E ratio of 25.

By comparison, the Standard & Poor's Corp. 500-stock index had an estimated 10% growth rate for 1992 and traded at a P-E of 18 based on '92 projected earnings. The manager, therefore, figured he was paying only a 40% premium to obtain 2.5 times the growth of the market.

"We're fundamentalists," Arends says. "We're always forward-looking in our analysis. Over time, don't forget that the best bargains are the best fundamental stories. Stocks that look expensive at current prices turn out to be the best over time."

Low Interest Rates

In an environment of low interest rates and low inflation, some managers are willing to pay even more for a company's earnings.

The market is at fair value when the earnings yield on the market equals the yield on a comparable fixed-income investment, according to Easton Ragsdale, chief quantitative analyst at Kidder, Peabody & Co.

If the one-year Treasury bill yields 4%, fair value would be a P-E of 25, he says. If the yield was 5%, a fair P-E would be 20 and, if it was 6%, a fair P-E would be 17%.

Paul Secord, manager of the Boston-based John Hancock Growth Fund, another A+ portfolio, generally likes to buy a stock when the ratio of the current year's estimated P-E relative to its growth rate is 0.75-to-1.

For example, if a company has a growth rate of 40%, he likes to buy that stock at a P-E of 30.

With interest rates low, however, Secord will buy a stock trading with a P-E relative to its growth rate of 1-to-1 to 1.5-to-1 times. Therefore, a growth stock with an estimated P-E relative to its growth rate of 1.0 times is "cheap compared to the market," Secord reckons.

As long as interest rates remain low, P-Es on growth stocks should remain high and the stocks should continue to perform well, according Stephen Poling, chief investment officer at Minneapolis-based and A+ rated Fortis Advisers Inc., formerly AMEV Advisers Inc.

There are even times when a big company justifies paying a higher multiple, notes William Berger, manager of the A+ rated Berger 100 Fund in Denver.

Big Companies

Large companies such as Wal-Mart and American Home Products Corp., he says, offer more stable and reliable earnings than smaller firms because their size offers greater diversification, deeper management and more thorough accounting analysis.

Timing Transactions

To Every Buy And Sell, There's A Day—And An Hour

■ **Selling on Fridays instead of on Mondays increased annual profit by 15%.**

When investing in stocks, the best strategy usually is not to run with the crowd. But because of the strong pull of emotions, notably fear and greed, many investors often march in lock-step with others and fail to buy or sell at the best time.

There are right and wrong times to buy and sell. Many savvy players know, for instance, that Mondays are generally down days and therefore represent a good chance to pick up stocks a few cents cheaper.

The 1929 stock market crash, which ushered in the Great Depression, happened on Monday, Oct. 28. It amounted to a drop of 12.8% in the Dow Jones industrial average and was followed by an 11.7% plunge the next day.

The Oct. 19, 1987, plunge, an even more staggering 22.6% drop, also occurred on a Monday that's now referred to as "Black Monday." The Dow has yet to undercut that day's close.

Market Patterns

Researchers have detected a pattern to the market's daily movement. The market tends to move higher after Mondays. The other four trading days have an upward bias with Wednesdays and Fridays historically the best.

A study by D. Keim and R. Stambaugh covering 1928 to 1982 found the Standard & Poor's composite index declined an average 0.18% on Mondays but rose 0.05% on Tuesdays, 0.10% on Wednesdays, 0.06% on Thursdays and 0.11% on Fridays.

Of course, historic patterns don't necessarily hold true over any given short span. In a study of the 12 months ended in January 1988, a period during which the S&P 500 rose 14.4%, *Investor's Business Daily* found a slightly different pattern. On Mondays, the S&P posted an average gain of 0.11%, a turn-around from its historic pattern.

Tuesdays were the best day of the week for the market during the same period, scoring an average increase of 0.28%. They were followed by Fridays with 0.23% and Wednesdays with 0.08%. Thursdays were poorest, rising only 0.03%.

But historically, selling on prior Fridays instead of on Mondays still would have increased average annual profit by almost 15%.

Friday Bulls

Thus, if an individual has already decided to sell a stock, it's better to do so on a Friday rather than waiting over the weekend. Conversely, even though Mondays have been branded as a "Crash Day" and "Black Monday," they're one of the best days to buy stocks.

"One reason Mondays are usually down days is that a lot of negative news is announced after the close on Friday to allow time for the market to absorb it," says portfolio manager Kenneth Levy of Jacobs Levy Equity Management in Fairfield, N.J.

"Almost all of the announcements of the Ivan Boesky insider scandal were made after Friday closes," notes Levy. "Also, the steep market plunge during the Depression showed many drops on Mondays, and the historic 1987 tumble came almost entirely on the Mondays in October.

"A lot of the declines on Mondays have to do with psychology," Levy adds.

"People love to announce good news, such as earnings and favorable deals, early in the week so investors will notice it.

"On the other hand, bad news is put out late in the week. Therefore, the effect shows up in the stock market on Monday."

Another reason for Monday's bearishness, Levy says, is that

the cumulative effect of brokers' sales calls is typically felt later in the week.

"All week long, brokers are pushing stocks to be bought," he says. "So generally the decision to sell stock is arrived at by an individual on his own. A lot of thinking goes on over the weekend, when people have time to sit down and review their portfolios. As a result, a lot of sell decisions are arrived at during the weekend, and the orders are executed on Mondays."

Levy notes that several universities have conducted psychological research on games that seems to have some relevance to the market. The findings showed that in the final phase of a game, when there are only a few minutes left to play, people grow more excited. In the case of market games, they had a tendency to bid up prices.

Intraday Trading

An analysis of intraday trading patterns shows that on Mondays—a down day in general—the market averages usually decline in the first hour, flatten out during the day, dip in the final hour and then stage a sharp rally in the final 30 minutes.

During the other four days—traditionally up days—the market on average rises in the first hour, levels out during the day (except for a brief dip during lunch in New York) and then moves sharply higher in the last hour.

The rise in prices late in the day may be traced to specialists' balancing their books or short-sellers' covering, Levy says. The closing price is important, he says, because it's used to calculate portfolio value. So, there may be some buying near the close to "paint the tape."

To exploit the pattern of market behavior on a daily and hourly basis, you would in theory take a long position on Monday in the last hour and sell on Fridays near the close.

But Levy says a problem facing a small investor would be transaction costs.

Instead, an indirect approach may be better. For example, those using a dollar averaging method of buying stocks could try to make their investments on Mondays. When they sell it could be on Fridays.

In any case, investors should be aware of the daily and hourly rhythm of the market so orders to buy and sell stock can be timed to their advantage.

Good Publicity

A Time To Review Your Holdings

■ **It's more than just coincidence that many top-performing issues top out about the time big stories are done on them.**

When money manager Arthur Bonnel saw the March 9, 1992, cover of *Business Week*, he knew it was time to sell his position in The Gap Inc.

The Gap already had been showing signs of wear after a fourfold run-up in 1991. In fact, the stock had topped in the second week of January.

But when the magazine did its positive story on the retail chain, following similarly upbeat articles in other major publications, it was the last straw.

Even after the favorable publicity, The Gap's stock continued to weaken as the company signaled slower sales and earnings ahead, and Bonnel felt things would get worse before they got better.

And so they did. The Gap was already 25% off its highs when the *Business Week* story ran. By the time the stock bottomed eight months later, it had lost 53% of its value.

Not all stocks end up the way The Gap did once the media fall in love with them.

Continuing Superior Performance

Loads of positive publicity, for example, on Home Depot Inc.—the greatest stock of the last decade—served only to highlight the continuing superior performance of the home-improvement chain. And biotechnology leader Amgen Inc. rose for years amid a continuous flow of positive articles.

But it's more than a coincidence that many top-performing

issues top out about the time big stories are done on them.

At the very least, investors who own such stocks should take flurries of publicity as a cue to review their positions.

In The Gap's case, while the company was being fawned over by one publication after another, its Relative Strength—which measures its stock performance against that of all other issues—was deteriorating badly.

Moreover, Gap's earnings, though still strong in early 1992, had established a pattern of deceleration. That is, starting with the second quarter of 1991, the company reported increases as follows: 93%, 71%, 52% and 48%.

By the time Gap posted only a 10% profit gain for its fiscal second quarter, most of the stock's decline was already out of the way. (Fiscal third-quarter earnings were down 14%.)

Because reported profit gains were still strong relative to other companies', the deceleration was not reflected early in The Gap's Earnings Per Share rank.

Its EPS pulled back from the high 90s in January to the still-respectable high-80s by springtime. It wasn't until after the second quarter's big earnings deceleration was reported that the EPS plunged into the 20s.

Relative Strength, however, was sounding the alarm much earlier. From 94 in early January, the RS had fallen to 83 by the end of that month and to a suspicious 73 by mid-February. Eventually, it sank to the 20s.

Generally speaking, stock-market leaders cease to be leaders when their Relative Strengths fall below 80.

High Point

A flood of good publicity often marks a high point for a company's stock, said Bonnel, who runs the MIM Stock Appreciation Fund in Reno, Nev. "Frequently, the main move has taken place on the stock once the press covers it," he says.

Karen McGrath, chief investment officer at National Investment Services of America, a Milwaukee-based institutional money management firm, concurs.

"Everything about the company is usually already known by the time the big stories come out," she says. "The odds are there will be no more positive surprises."

The January 1992 peak in biotech stocks, for example, coincided with several bullish articles about the group, McGrath notes.

"The bottom line is that publicity is like a spotlight," said Jonathan Schoolar, co-manager of the AIM Weingarten and Constellation funds in Houston. "It's great if you're a super-performer. But if a stock's in the spotlight and it doesn't perform, they'll throw a lot of cabbages at you.

"I use the publicity as a way to remind me that this is a company to pay close attention to and make sure it continues to perform," Schoolar says.

Home Depot is an example of a "superperformer," he said.

"It got a lot of press (in 1992), but earnings remained strong. They came in better than expected and were at least a penny better than expected for five quarters," he recalled. "There's a situation where a stock's got a lot of press, but I didn't sell because earnings continued to come through."

Double-Checking

Money managers concur that after a surge of publicity, it may be time to check to see that fundamental reasons for the initial purchase of the stock remain intact.

"You need to keep your finger close to the trigger," Schoolar says, especially if good publicity is accompanied by insider selling.

Bonnel keeps an extra close eye on those stocks he owns that get a lot of positive publicity. If they don't act well, and if it appears investors are using the good press to take profits, he will consider taking profits himself.

Just as good press can be a signal to consider selling, bad press can be an opportunity to contemplate buying, money managers also say.

Schoolar remembers scooping up Wal-Mart Stores Inc. after the late founder Sam Walton was reported critically ill. The stock opened off 10% that day, he recalled, and he bought "a bunch" at $33 a share. The stock was touching 60 a little over a year later. "The (Walton) news," he said, "was sheerly emotional."

Schoolar also seized an opportunity to buy Wal-Mart in October 1990 after yet another analyst declared the stock "overvalued" in a Wall Street Journal article.

(Many experts have declared Wal-Mart "overvalued" in the last 20 years, a period during which the stock has appreciated 18,000%, give or take a few hundred percent.)

Schoolar has also used negative publicity to pick up Philip Morris Cos., which has gotten kicked around from time to time when tobacco-liability lawsuits are in the news.

If a negative article is published about a company that he continues to like (after taking the negative news into account), Schoolar uses the bad publicity as a buying opportunity.

Bonnel is happy if his holdings never get any ink. And he's especially wary when the praise he hears for companies or stocks is coming from the mouths of neighbors and acquaintances in supermarkets or at cocktail parties. That's his signal to stay away—far away.

Mutual Funds

Mutual Fund Snapshots

Peering Into The Pros' Portfolios

■ **If top funds are unloading a stock you own, it's a good time to review your reasons for hanging on to it.**

Keeping tabs on what stocks professional investors are buying—and selling—can help individual investors separate the leaders from the laggards.

One source of keen insight into the pros' activity is the mutual fund coverage provided by *Investor's Business Daily*.

Each day, the investment activity of six top-performing funds is dissected and spread out for readers' inspection. Summaries of each fund's 10 largest investments as well as its top new buys and sells in the most recent quarter are provided.

Similar Holdings

Of particular note are the similarities you will often find among the best funds' holdings.

Consider, for example, the overlap of the funds profiled in November 1992 and shown on the next page. Cisco Systems Inc., a manufacturer of computer networking equipment that had made a 13-fold move from its October 1990 low, was the biggest holding of both John Hancock Special Equities and 20th Century Ultra.

20th Century Ultra was shown in the most recent reporting period to have bought 2.8 million shares of International Game Technology Inc., a maker of gambling equipment that had soared 18-fold since October 1990. During the same time, Enterprise Capital Appreciation accumulated 18,000 shares.

Enterprise Capital's largest holding was U.S. Healthcare Inc., which also was a big position in the AIM Constellation Fund.

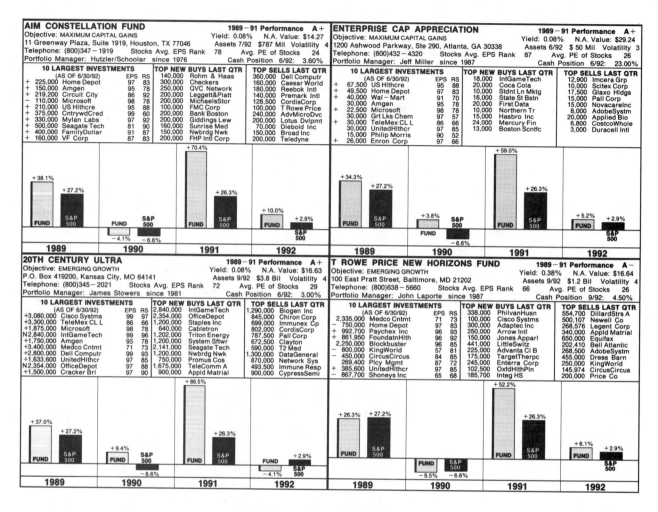

AIM Constellation's largest position was in Home Depot Inc., which also happened to be the second biggest holding of T. Rowe Price's New Horizons fund.

In addition, Amgen Inc. and Microsoft Corp. were major positions of three funds.

Divergent Opinions

But while great minds often think alike, they often have differing opinions.

While 20th Century Ultra was adding to its stake in Dell Computer Inc., AIM Constellation sold 360,000 shares. But both were accumulating positions in Newbridge Networks Corp., a Canadian telecommunications firm whose stock had quadrupled since the start of the year.

Reviewing Your Holdings

If a couple of top funds are shown to be unloading a stock you also own, it might be a good time to review your reasons for hanging on to it. The best fund managers get to the top by staying ahead of the crowd, not only in their buying but also in their selling.

For example, T. Rowe Price New Horizon fund sold 268,500 shares of software developer Adobe Systems Inc. at the same time Enterprise Capital Appreciation was selling its position. Adobe had been trending lower since setting a high in early January.

Also, 20th Century Ultra unloaded more than 800,000 shares of Cordis Corp., a maker of medical instruments, while AIM Constellation was parting with 128,500 shares. Cordis' stock peaked in October 1991.

Mutual Fund Cash Position

A Market Store Of Dry Powder

■ A cash level of 12% or higher is bullish and a level of 9% or lower is bearish.

Cash levels in stock funds represent potential new purchases of equities.

Many stock funds are allowed to keep a substantial amount of assets in cash or equivalents, such as money market instruments or short-term Treasury securities.

A fund's cash level climbs when money flows into the fund and the portfolio manager is unwilling to buy additional stocks. Heavy inflows often occur after a run-up in stock prices, when a fund's current holdings exceed buy levels and the manager can find few new attractive prospects.

In addition, most fund managers keep some cash on hand to accommodate any real or expected redemptions.

Extreme Levels

Philip Roth, chief technical analyst at Dean Witter Reynolds Inc., says he views a cash level of 12% or higher as bullish and a level of 9% or lower as bearish. Those levels represent extremes rarely reached in the past 15 years, he notes.

"It dropped under 8% early in 1992, and for all intents and purposes that was a peak of some kind," he said.

Funds' cash level increased from January, reaching 9.9% in August. But it slipped in September to 9.3%.

"I interpret this to mean that as there was some buildup in caution on the part of portfolio managers in the second and third quarters, they built up a little buying power," Roth said. "In September, they decided to start putting it back in."

Mutual Fund Cash Position

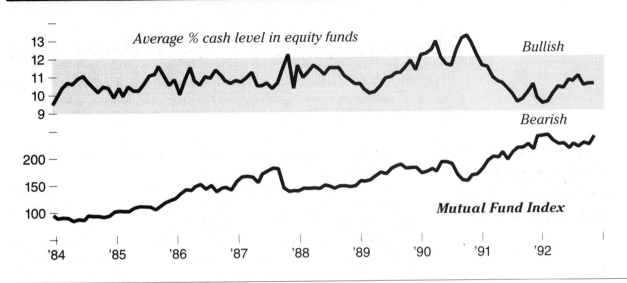

Roth says the cash level gave a negative signal in early 1992, which has improved but has yet to be reversed.

Roth observed that the huge influx of money into equity funds this year enabled cautious portfolio managers to raise cash levels without having to sell positions. A record $58.01 billion in net new cash flow was dumped into equity funds through September, according to the Investment Company Institute.

If new money hadn't been pouring into the equity funds and portfolio managers needed to sell stocks in order to reach desired cash levels, Roth said, "it obviously would have had a much different effect on the market."

Low Interest Rates

Interest rates play a role in cash levels. With banks paying less than 3% on savings accounts, money has flowed into money market funds en route to mutual funds. A significant rise in rates could "cut off the cash flow into equity funds, which would have an adverse effect on stocks," Roth said.

The supply of new stock coming on the market in the form of initial public offerings also plays a part in cash-level dynamics. For example, the market might get along fine with small amounts of cash waiting on the sidelines if the supply of new stocks were low.

But as IPOs have picked up, the market has needed a relatively greater amount of cash ready to swallow additional supply.

Some money managers are more impressed by the absolute amount of dollars in funds' liquid assets than the percentage of total assets represented by cash.

Rod Linafelter, co-manager of Berger 100 Fund, is one who puts less emphasis on percentage. "It's meaningless. It's not percentages that make the market go up, it's the absolute amount."

He may have a point. The amount of money in liquid assets was $39.48 billion on Sept. 30, 1992, when the percentage was 9.3%. That compares with $29.15 billion waiting in cash in funds on Oct. 30, 1990, when the level was 12.9% of equity funds' total assets.

Roth also considers the absolute numbers, but insists the percentages are more useful.

Investors also may find it helpful to look at how cash positions are spread among different types of equity funds. As of Sept. 30, 1992, aggressive growth funds led in cash positions with 11.5%, or $7.82 billion, while growth-and-income funds were running at 7.5% cash, or $11.54 billion. Growth funds had 10.6% of assets in cash, or $13.8 billion.

Index